These Wonderful People

Reza Kianian

© Firouz Media 2023
All rights reserved

All rights reserved by the publisher. No parts of this publication may be reproduced, stored in a retrieval system, or transmitted in any form or by any means, electronic, mechanical, photocopying, recording, or otherwise, without the prior permission of the publisher.

Title: These Wonderful People
Author: Reza Kianian
Trasnlated by: Niloufar Madjlessi

ISBN 9781915557025
eISBN 9781915557032

Firouz Media Limited
www.firouzmedia.com
IG: @firouzmedia

*With profound appreciation, we extend our special thanks to Reza Kianian, Masoud Pakdel, Payam Eraee, and Reza Moataria who contributed to the publication of this book.

Author's note:

To Hayedeh

For all the days and nights she was unable
To walk in the streets with her husband
Alone and relaxed.
For all the moments she was unable
To be alone with her husband
In restaurants, coffee shops, cinemas, theatres, and gatherings.

Close-Up

It was after the television series "Apartment", written by Farhad Tohidi, directed by Asghar Hashemi, produced by Behrouz Khoshrazm, and a production manager who never paid my last installment, that I became famous.

People knew me now and at times called me by my name. One day, as I left the offices of the "Film Report" magazine and started walking down Keshavarz Blvd towards Laleh Park walking past Tous Street, three high school girls recognised me and started screaming! That magical moment was finally here. The girls screamed as they set eyes on me. It made me happy. Very much so. Fame had found me. I walked along the pavement and degusted fame carefully. It was sweet. I began to daydream as I always do. I travelled into the future. To more fame. More and more. And then, I asked myself: "Is this what you wanted?" I paused briefly in my mind and weighed the answers. Finally, I came up with: "No! Certainly not! If this is what I wanted, I'd have to see what the people want and follow that path. I'd have to see what those girls so good at screaming liked and reacted to that. But I like what I want. My own liking is more important to me. It was not just fame I was after. I wanted to be an actor; and if it made me famous into the bargain, so much the better. My choice was to portray different characters. I did not want to stay prisoner to playing the same character over and over. I did not want to stay in the prison of what the audience wanted. I had a decision to make. I had made my decision and I had to stick to it. What the audience wants is alluring. I mustn't surrender. It reminded me of Ulysses when he was approaching the island of the seductive sirens. He ordered his ship's crew to tie him to the mast and not let him go no matter —

how much he yelled until they had sailed past the island. I must not allow myself to be seduced. —I was outside the Boulevard cinema when I tied myself to the mast.

Many years have passed since that day. I have played many characters. I am also famous. But a new seduction comes my way every day. I must stay close to the ship's mast, always. I must continue my acting career.

Fame steals your secluded space. All eyes are on you wherever you go. They are there with you wherever you go. You are under the magnifying glass. Home is the only place to be alone; and even then, only if phone calls by fans let you! When at home, the curtains must always be shut. Interested neighbours are also numerous. I need space like any other being. I need solitude too. In acting, there is no seclusion in any shape or form. A performer has company on stage and off stage. He is never alone… And what could I do as a person who likes his solitude and loves acting beyond love? Outside of acting, and outside my social life, I decided to write. I finally sat down and wrote and became a writer. Later on, I made sculptures too. I also take pictures these days, and I paint. I was able to create my secluded space and hold on to my acting and fans too. I love the people. I love crowds. I love seclusion. And now, I have it all. Thank God.

I have a home in many hearts. I will never be homeless. I will never be without a roof over my head. All the hearts, all the blood, all the throbbing. So much love, so much solitude, and so many people. These wonderful people.

Michael Caine once said that a family of three Iranians recognised him when he was strolling along the Thames one day. They are delighted. They walk up to him and ask him for a photo by expressing their indescribable happiness. He agrees. The father of the family hands the camera to Caine and the three of them stand with their backs to the river and say: "We're ready. Take the picture!" This sort of thing happen to all actors, including me.

It has been a while since I decided to write my memoirs and

publish them. You are holding them in your hands now. I have forgotten many, and there are many that cannot be published, so they are not in this book. What you are reading is not in chronological order. They move back and forth in time. It is not important. What is more important is the moral of the story. During this time, I have jotted down my every interesting encounter with the people and tried to remember past memories too. In any case, everything I remembered and everything which was publishable is in this diary.

I hope to publish other diaries in the years to come, but who knows how much time I have left. The title for the present book was chosen by Houshang Golmakani. When I sent some of these memoirs to the Film Report magazine for publication in their spring edition a couple of years ago, I had no title for them. Houshang Golmakani suggested this title. I am grateful to him.

Night – Outdoors – Around the City Theatre, Tehran

I was going to see a play. I parked the car in one of the back alleys around the City Theatre and started putting on the steering-wheel lock when two young men recognised me. One of them said: Reza Kianian. They walked up to me and said hello. I answered as I was finishing up my operation to stop my car from being burgled when I was gone; even though I had left the window open on occasion before.

They carried on with FAQs and I answered as I kept busy with the locking operation. I was in a rush. They left. I finished what I was doing and left for the theatre.

I was going to watch the "Backyard" by Chista Yasrebi. The youngsters walked in front of me and turned back to look at me a couple of times. I watched the play. Interesting piece of work. When I returned to my car, backtracking the entire operation, I saw the same two youngsters. I waved at them. They had been to see the "Backyard" too. They came up to me and we said hello again. One of them said: "Why were you so cold when we said hello to you?" I replied: "I was in a rush. I was also busy making the car safe."

"We were really upset when we left. I told my friend I'll never dig Kianian's work again. But I'll watch them now that you've warmed up to us", He said.

"You find it that simple to let go of someone and get back in there again!"

"Well, I was really into your works. I didn't expect you to be that cold … Especially in Bagh Ferdows, at five in the afternoon. I was so into those love scenes. It was just like the Last Tango! And you were like the great Marlon Brando!"

"But my love scenes were somewhat different from his, wouldn't you say!" I said.

He said: "I imagined the rest!" Adding: "The Last Tango in Paris." I know a thing or two about the movies.

And left.

Day – Outdoors – **Sanandaj**

We were staying in Sanandaj to shoot "The Familiar Soil" by Bahman Farmanara. I had gone to buy fruits on a day off. A young boy greeted me eagerly and asked for my autograph.

He said: "Welcome to our city. Although, I'm not from Sanandaj either. I'm a guest here too."

I thanked him. As I was signing his piece of paper, he said: "I really like your movie 'The Fish Die'." I've watched it over and over again. It's great. It's really good."

"You mean 'The Fish Fall in Love'?" I said.

"No. 'The Fish Die.'"

He took the singed piece of paper and left.

Day – Outdoors – **Sanandaj**

The young man stood facing me and laughing for having discovered me. I said hello to him.

"The guys reported that you're in Sanandaj. I got here as fast as I could." He said.

I exchanged pleasantries, and I started to walk. He walked with me.

He continued: "Is it alright if I walk with you?"

"Yes."

He did, and said: "Is it alright if I say something?"

"Please do."

"I wanted to ask you please not to play in ideological movies!"

I asked: "Like which ones?"

"The same ones those higher up want."

"Like which ones?"

"You know!"

I said: "But I'm not in your mind."

"For instance, the Kamkars who are the same townsfolk as us. They've recently released an album with … – he named someone I didn't know. This character is with those higher up."

"I'm sorry, I don't know him."

"Although I like the Kamkars, I don't agree with what they've done, because…"

And he carried on with the same bombast that I don't need to repeat here.

"But if you don't like people to tell you what to do, why would you want to be the boss of others? Why would you want others to think like you and be like you?'

"I said please."

"Don't you think you'd be giving orders instead of saying please if you were in a position of power?"

He paused for a second, "Maybe", adding that he believed in committed literature.

"Meaning what?"

He said: "Literature about freedom."

"Don't you think you're restraining freedom by using the term committed? By freedom you mean what you like?"

"You're too democratic."

"Is it bad?" I asked.

"I don't know. I have to think. But there's a limit to everything."

"Please allow everyone to be as they are."

Plagued by uncertainty now, he changed the subject and said he was reading sociology.

I remembered the 1970s.

Day – Outdoors – **Sanandaj**

I was outside, looking for a watch store to change the strap on mine. An excited youngster walked up to me, said hello, we exchanged pleasantries, and the rest of the story. Another two also joined us. They were his friends. Young people walking the streets on a Friday afternoon to pass the time of day; and they were happy and excited to see an actor at this carefree time. I was walking and they were following me. They asked if they could accompany me. I gave a positive rely. They came. A little later, they were done with the same old questions.

"I'm looking for a watch store to change the strap on mine."

They said: "We must go to Pasdaran Street. Uptown. What are you doing downtown."

"Uptowns all look the same everywhere now. Only downtowns are still slightly different." I said.

They found this interesting; it was like a discovery!

We carried on walking uptown towards Pasdaran Street. We arrived at a posh small town shopping centre in the same style of those in Tehran. Like one of those Tehran had copied from Dubai; and the people of Dubai from the Americans. We were oblivious to our own bazaars, which had been copied by the Europeans, and then copied by the Americans from them. They showed me a small watch store. Two people were sitting in it. They recognised me and were very welcoming. They placed a few black leather straps on the counter. I looked at the back.

"It's hypoallergenic." He said.

I selected one. He replaced it for me. I wanted him to put the old buckle on the new strap. He did not want to take my money, but I insisted and he did, filled with shame. "I'm sorry that this strap is not fit for you. But it'll do as a temporary one until you get back to Tehran."

"This is fine. What more could I ask for? My watch is not an expensive one." I said.

"Please, you're too modest."

I said no more. Just goodbye. He could not believe that I did not have an expensive watch. He had no idea how good I was at losing watches. The three youngsters kept apologising too and saying sorry there are no watch straps in Sanandaj which are fit for you!

Day – Outdoors – Bandar Anzali Port

We had all gathered at the pier for the movie by Saman Moghadam called "Miss Iran". Parviz Parastui and I were standing on either side of the set. A young man was chasing us. He wore glasses and had little vision. Every time he approached one of us, we had swapped places. He had such a hard time finding us. He found me at last and walked up to. I gave him my autograph and then he wanted to take a photo. I accepted. He went and fetched the tourist photographer from the port. The photographer was delighted to see me. The twinkle in his eye told me that he was queuing up customers in his mind to bring and take photos with me.

When the bloke with the glasses was ready, he placed one arm around my shoulder and said: "By the way, I have no money on me. Can you pay and then I'll pay you later."

Night – Indoors – Rose Club

We were shooting the sequence for the Rose Club for Saman Moghadam's film "Miss Iran". I had to dance in this scene; dance to Tom Jones's "She's a Lady", and then perform a "Mr Muscleman"[1] dance with the same song. The scene, however, was cut before screening. Before we started filming, I noticed a group of ladies who had come as guests. I recognised Leila Kelari among them. I went up to her and said hello. I saw Saman Moghadam's mother and said hello; and a number of other ladies – Saman's mother's kith and kin. I thought they had just dropped by to see Saman, but Leila said we've come to see you dance!

The night before, Mahmoud Kelari had told her that Reza will be dancing tomorrow. Saman had said the same thing to his mother. I was surprised, because I cannot dance. I can just mimic people here and there. I can pick up their rhythm and moves as they dance and imitate them. To do this scene, I'd watched an old

---

1- Iranian version of "Cockney" in downtown Tehran, usually called "Kolah Makhmali" or velvet hat.

Tom Jones show and I was going to imitate him in addition to the "Mr Muscleman" dance which was once performed by the belated popular actor, Fardin.

I said: "Well, I'm sorry you've come all this way to see me dance."

The scene was shot repeatedly due to the camera angle and other difficulties which arose. The audience got gradually tired and left, and I had to carry on soaking in sweat.

As dawn broke and shooting stopped, a few drama students came over, wished us well, and asked: "Where's your dance class? How much is the tuition and how long is each term?"

It's the tradition these days; everyone teaches a class. To see someone close-up, you must enroll in their classes and pay the fee.

"I don't have any classes", I said.

They said: "Oh! What a shame. Please organise one."

"Well, I'm a classless person."

Night – Outdoors – Outside My House

It was nine o'clockish at night when I got home. I had not had time to take my shoes off when the doorbell rang. I picked up the handset and asked who it was. Someone answered: "Mr Kianian, would you mind coming down for a second please. I've been waiting here for you for hours now."

I had noticed him as I was driving into the garage. I get visitors every now and then. I went to the door. He was a boney young man, around thirtyish.

"I don't want to become an actor, I don't want to see you from close-up, and I don't want an autograph." He said.

"Please tell me what you want."

After many apologies for the inconvenience, he said: "I've been trying to put on weight for a long time now. But I simply can't. A few days ago, I got the CD of the film "A House Built on Water". I went home and watched it. I was surprised to see you had put on so much weight. Afterwards, I found out that you had put on 20kgs for the film. I've been trying to put on some weight for a long time now, but I can't no matter what I do. Please help me out and give me diet. If you can give me medication, that's fine too; I don't care about the cost!"

After screening "A House Built on Water", the same thing happened to me several times in different ways. Everyone wanted my advice – but mostly women, and mostly to lose weight!

Day – Indoors – Taxi

After the series "Apartment", when I had just become famous, I got into a taxi in Enghelab Sq. I was going towards Bahar Street. As usual, one or two ladies recognised me, said hello, and wanted to know how the series would end.

In the meantime, the driver also recognised me. His looks in the mirror were interesting. Every time he looked, it was as if he made a new discovery and a soft smile ran under his skin.

The ladies got off in Ferdowsi Sq. There was just me and him now.

"Please, come and sit in the front." He said.

I did. There was something he wanted to say, but kept hesitating. Finally, he said: "Thinking of her as a sister, the lady who plays the part of your wife is very pretty."

"Yes, she's married with two daughters."

He fell silent. He did not pick up any more passengers. He kept looking at me as if he wanted to say something, but then wouldn't.

"Please let me off at the top of Bahar Street." I said.

He realised that there was no more time left to say what had occupied his mind from the start. At the same time as he pressed on the brakes, he asked: "By the way Mr Kianian, what's the corruption like in the film business?"

Day – Indoors – Courthouse

I had a stubborn and rude prank caller. I finally had enough. I went to the phone exchange and said I have a prank caller. They gave me a code to enter in the phone every time he called so they could cut him off. I took the code and asked for a list of his calls so that I could also make a complaint. They said I needed a court warrant. So I went to the courthouse, placed my complaint, and waited to be admitted into the judge's chambers.

Two interesting things happened as I waited.

1. A young man, who was arguing with his wife and had come to get a divorce, kept hovering around me. Finally, he walked up to me and asked without beating about the bush: "My wife wants a divorce. I love her and I can't live without her. Please, can you mediate and get her off her high horse."

"I understand, but what can I do in the middle of all this?"

"My wife adores you. She'll listen to you if you talk to her."

He kept pleading. I finally accepted. I asked him to stay away. I went to his wife and said hello. She looked up. She had a black eye and a swollen lip which had split open. She had been battered. I hate men who batter their wives. I feel the same way about parents who hit their children. Those who abuse their power churn my stomach, because they have no logic; because they abuse their naturally superior strength.

The woman was happy, because her anger and the sadness in her eyes vanished and a mild smile ran under her battered skin. She cried. The lump in her throat burst and the floodgates opened. She said sobbing: "This twat keeps hitting me. He does it all the time. I hate his guts."

And she cried.

I said: "I'm sorry that you can't get divorced that easily. He can make you run around until your hair turns white. You won't get anywhere with your complaint."

"I won't go back to him."

"I have a good solution for you if you'll listen."

"I won't go back to him."

"Fine, fine. Just listen."

She stared at me with a battered face soaked in tears.

"Tell him you'll go back home only if he grants you the right to divorce."

She could not understand at first. I explained the whole thing in detail. I talked and said if she had the right to divorce, she could stand up to his bullying. She finally understood and accepted.

I signalled at the young man to come over. "Your wife has accepted to come back home."

The man was happy. He took my hand to kiss it, but I pulled it back. I browbeat him for abusing his physical strength. I made him promise he would not hit his wife again. He wanted to take her home when she said: "On one condition."

"I'll do anything." The man said firmly.

"I'll take back my complaint and come home if you officially give me the right to divorce at the registry office."

The man's excitement died down a bit. He looked pensive.

I said: "Why are you thinking? Do you want to hit your wife again?"

"No, no, as God is my witness."

"Fine then, there's no need to think." I said.

"You're right." He turned to his wife: "Let's go to the registry office."

I turned around to see if my turn had come.

2. I saw a big, overweight man who was wearing a long, white cotton shirt and trousers. The shirt had a round collar and was slit on the sides. He had a green taqiyah on his head and a green shawl around his neck. A few large agate and turquoise rings made his chubby fingers look even chubbier. A pair of kalash shoes from the western Kermanshah region adorned his feet. His thick beard was white and well groomed. He talked in a loud voice with an aggressive tone and volume. I started observing him in my same acting habit when I begin to analyse and register all the moves, postures, and appearances of anyone new I see. He noticed and recognised me. Suddenly, he hugged me like a little chick and kissed me. He smelled of rose water. "What are you doing here?"

"It's nothing." I said.

"Never mind the courts and all that. Whatever it is, you can tell hour humble servant. I'll send some of the gang on motorbike to sort it out. The b*****ds…"

In the space of a few minutes, he told me that he had helped many artists, especially actors, after the revolution. He named a few actresses who worked before the revolution that he had saved from being executed by making them into his concubines and taking charge. He also named a few female singers who worked before the revolution who had also become his concubines and were saved from death, annihilation, and execution. It sounded as if all the women were going to be hanged! And now he was offering me his help! Someone stepped out of one of the rooms. He let go of me and walked towards him, threatening him in the same loud, aggressive voice. Then he left him alone and walked back towards me. He gave me a phone number and said: "Anywhere, and I mean anywhere you get stuck, just call your haji and give me the guy's details. I'll send the gang to give him a good dressing down. I'm your humble servant Mr Reza. Dig us. We're a lout with a credo."

Day – Night – Outdoors – Streets of Tehran

It has often happened that I've become angry behind the wheel when someone has committed an offense. For instance, when they drive through a red light, speed onto the main road from a side street, go down a one-way street, or double-park their car and block the street. I get mad and honk my horn or don't give way. Those offenders I'm objecting to tell me: "Why you? You're a role model in society; why're you honking your horn? Why won't you let us pass? Why are you protesting?"

Night – Outdoors – Anzali Port

One night, after we had finished shooting for "The Fish Fall in Love", we went to one of the booths in the boulevard next to the pier with Roya Nonahali to sit and talk. After a few minutes had passed, the tourist photographer of the boulevard noticed us. Those days, the "Sleep and Wake" series in which Roya had played was being aired and many called her by her character's name "Natasha"! The photographer came up to us and asked if he could take our picture. I asked for Roya's permission. She agreed, the photographer took the picture, thanked us and left. We were still talking when he returned.

"I'm really sorry, I do apologise, one of the guys here wants to take a picture with you. Can he do that please?" He said.

Roya agreed. The photographer positioned the young man next to us, took the picture, thanked us, and both of them left. He returned a bit later with a smile on his face, saying: "I'm sorry, I do apologise, these two people also want a picture with you."

They were a young couple. They took their picture and left.

The same thing kept happening until we decided it would be best to continue our conversation at the hotel where we were staying with the crew. A little further down the road, we saw the photographer and heard him shout in the crowd: "Take a picture with Natasha for a thousand tomans. A photo with Natasha for a thousand tomans."

Day – Indoors – Airplane

We were on our way to Mashhad with Hayedeh and Ali. A young girl was sitting in the seat next to me. From the start, it was obvious that she was happy about sitting next to me. It was obvious from her gentle smiles and fleeting peeks. She kept fidgeting in her seat and trying to start a conversation at any price.

Eventually, once the crew had served us and was clearing up, the girl snatched my tray and gave it to attendant. I thanked her, and she continued … After all the usual chitchat, she said: "I know where you live." I found it interesting and asked: "Where?" She said: "Zafaranieh".

I did not tell her my home was not in Zafaranieh.

She continued: "I even know what your house looks like." And she described every little detail of the house in Zafaranieh; a mansion with a floor area of 1,500 m^2 in the midst of the grounds. It had many halls and rooms and staircases, and…

Day – Outdoors – Street

We were shooting a scene for the film "The Cinema is the Cinema". Our cameraman was adjusting the lighting. Like always, he brought the light metre up to my face, looked at the digits, and left.

A few shots were taken.

When it got to the shot where I had nothing to do, I stood to one side. One of the people who had abandoned their work to watch us edged his way through the crowd towards me and asked in a low voice: "What's this instrument they hold under your nose to smell before the shooting then?"

He was talking about the light metre.

Day – Indoors – Outdoors – Rouzbeh Hospital

We were shooting at the Rouzbeh Hospital for the mentally ill for a few days for the series "Sarnakh" [The Clue] by Kiumars Pourahmad. Moderate mentally ill patients are hospitalised and treated here. The patients are either cured and discharged, or else they get worse and are referred to Aminabad.

During those few days there, I tried to make contact and spend time with them. The nurses also helped me out and took me to different wards. I had a packet of cigarettes on me which I occasionally offered to patients on the approval of the nurses. They all craved cigarettes and smoked with voracity. Except this one young man who did not ask me for any. Even when I offered him some, he just laughed and twisted the elastic hem of his pajamas. Inside it, all around his waist was filled with cigarettes. He said: "Let me know anytime you want one."

One of the nurses took me to the women's ward. It was much sadder than the men's ward. Some of the girls and women saw me and two of them recognised me. They ran towards me to kiss me! I hid behind the nurses. The nurses stopped them and forced them to go back to their rooms. They explained that the sedatives injected into patients stimulated the women and took the steam out of the men.

About an hour later, I was sitting in the courtyard and talking to the same young man who had cigarettes in the hem of his pajamas. I noticed that one of those girls was slowly and stealthily coming towards me from behind the trees. She had escaped the ward just to kiss me. Her eyes were filled with lust and restlessness. I looked around for a nurse to restrain her. Fortunately, one of the nurses was walking past, but the girl attacked before I could call her. The young man grabbed her and the nurse came and took her away. She turned around and took another look at me with a sick, frightened smile as she was being warded off.

I had to play the part of a person who had pleaded insanity to escape the law. The police were suspicious of him and questioning him in that same hospital.

The part of the police officer was being played by Jahanbakhsh Soltani. He was standing over my bed in my room and was asking me some questions. And I kept asking him if he had any cigarettes. I had seen this at the hospital and suggested it to Pourahmad who agreed to it.

As we shot the scene, I could see from my window that a group of patients were peeping and watching, including that same young man who was hoarding cigarettes!

The police officer kept asking me all sorts of questions, and I just kept asking: "Got any cigarettes?"

At once, the door opened and the same young man approached, saying: "Why do you keep begging this one? Didn't I tell you to come to me any time you wanted a fag." He took a few cigarettes out of the hem of his pajamas and placed them in front of me. He gave glaring sideway glances at Jahanbakhsh Soltani and exited.

It was a great shame that Javanrouh did not shoot the scene.

Day – Outdoors – Indoors – Tehran

We were going to our local video club with Davoud Amiri to hire some CDs. Just as we were about to go in, a biker parked on the pavement outside the shop door as usual. The passengers were a man, a woman, and a child in the woman's arms. The man walked into the shop shortly after us. He recognised me, we said hello, exchanged pleasantries… After much talking, he had completely forgotten why he had even come to the shop. As we walked out, he said to me: "Please, would you say hello to our kids," meaning his wife and child. "They'll be thrilled."

Day – Outdoors – Sanandaj

I was walking on Enghelab Street and looking around. A young man walked up to me and said hello. He was obviously a bookworm with his spick-and-span literary lexicon. I suggested we walk together. He was happy and we started along. He asked about the situation in the cinema and theatre, and complained about the book situation. He said he had written a screenplay and what he should do with it. Who to give it to and where? He said he had a series of stories which were also good for screenplays. It was decided that he should take them to the House of Cinema and register them there.

I had to get back. I said goodbye and told him to contact me if he was in Tehran so we could meet up. He said he did not think he would come to Tehran, because he worked at the radio and wrote for them; that he was so busy he was sure he could not make it to Tehran.

I am not sure why he asked for the address of the House of Cinema.

Day – Indoors – My House

My mother, may she rest in peace, had arrived from Mashhad and was giving out the gifts she had brought for us. The beloved saffron, barberry, and dried Bokhara plums…

Only this time, she had also brought me a T-shirt. She said: "When I'd gone with my sister Marzieh to shop for the children, we saw this T-shirt and my sister said to buy it for Reza." Then, they had started haggling with the shopkeeper, who had not budged an inch. In the end, my mother had said do you know who I am buying this for? Reza Kianian! And the shopkeeper had given them a discount. He had also given them a discount on the other items of clothing and said to say hello. My mother added: "I must go shopping with you from now on." And she never did.

Nobody is respected for their social status beyond the grave anymore. In that other world, my mother must do me the favours as his son.

Day – Indoors – A Mall on Kish Island

We had travelled to Kish Island with Hayedeh, Ali, Mani, Auntie Pari, Jamileh… We were busy shopping in one of the malls. The ladies were looking at clothes and home appliances, and Ali and I were looking for a camera. Ali wanted to buy a camera. Ali and I bought the camera in no time at all and then started to look around and laugh at this and that until we were bored and started looking for the ladies. We found them in a boutique. We walked in and the shopkeeper was overjoyed when he saw me. He came up to us and chitchatted a bit, then made his apologies and said he had to serve his customers. I went to the ladies who were haggling insistently – but only Mani, Hayedeh's mother, and Auntie Pari. The shopkeeper apologised to me again.

"Don't worry. I'm with these ladies. My wife, mother-in-law, aunt, cousin…"

The shopkeeper became interested and gave a good discount all-around. I joked: "You made a mistake. If I tell you who these ladies are, you must give another discount too."

"Who are they?" He asked.

The shopkeeper was a polite young man and into poetry, because he had hung beautifully calligraphed verses from contemporary poets around his shop, including Sohrab Sepehri.

"These two ladies (pointing to Mani and Auntie Pari) are the sisters of Sohrab Sepehri.

He was so thrilled that he wanted to give away the clothes. Everything was topsy-turvy now. Mani and Auntie Pari insisted that the shopkeeper take the money!

Day – Indoors – Aminabad Asylum

We were going to Aminabad with Siamak Shayeghi at five in the afternoon to shoot a scene for the movie "Ferdows Gardens". We were working in the women's ward. Those poor people were injected with medication twice a day to keep them sedated.

One girl and a middle-aged woman attracted my attention more than the rest. The girl was around twenty. She talked to herself, walked around, and would suddenly crouch in a corner petrified, asking for help … Next, she would be laughing a horse laugh.

I asked the warden: "What's her story?"

"Her father, brother, and maternal uncle have raped her."

That was enough. I did not want to hear the rest.

As for the woman, she was around fifty. A distinguished woman of good descent. She had salt-and-pepper hair and carried herself with panache. One day, before she was injected with her morning medication and still had her wits about her, she said hello to me. It was clear from the way she talked that she was an educated person. She asked me if it was possible for me to get her a suitable scarf, manteau, and socks. I said yes and she walked away quickly not to attract attention.

That night, I told Hayedeh what had happened and she sorted out a suitable scarf, manteau, and socks for her.

I found her before the injections the next morning and gave her the package. She thanked me profusely. I asked her why she was there.

Terrified, she said: "They've murdered my husband!" She added that he was all she had. She said that she was a relative of a playwright.

"I know him." I said.

She was not listening. In a rush, she continued by saying that her relatives had come over from Canada and thrown her into the asylum, because they want to rip her off of her husband's inheritance. She said they called this place and told them that I am crazy, and these people transferred me here in an ambulance.

… Duty called. I left. She was also taken for her injection around the same time … What she said was something between madness and the truth. I did not know whether I should believe her not. I thought would i go bonkers too if they injected me with those medicines!?

During my break there, I called the playwright. His mobile was off. I called at night too, but it was still off. I asked a mutual friend who said: "He's not in Iran. He's gone abroad for a play!"

The next morning, I went to see that lady before her injections. She had asked me to keep her in the picture. I told her her relative was not in Iran. She was devastated. She gave the number of a more distant relative and said to call them and ask them to come and take her out of that place. She said she would go mad there and repeated that her husband had been murdered! She said they wanted to sell her house and rip her off; that they had bought their tickets and would be returning to Canada in a fortnight, and she would have to spend the rest of her life in the asylum…

In-between the shootings, I'd ask the nurses about her. They would say she is not well and talks gibberish. Her husband had died; he had not been murdered … She walked past me and did not even recognise me. She was staring at something, perhaps in the depths of her mind. Every night, I would recount the events of that day for Hayedeh. Hayedeh said to call the number of the other relative too. I did. When I introduced myself, they were both happy and surprised that I had called them. They thought perhaps it was a TV programme. When I told them the story, there was silence. Silence … mumbling … They were not happy to talk about it. Finally, one of the ladies at the other end of the line told me: "She's telling the truth" and asked me not to get her involved in the story. They did not wish to discuss the situation any further and said goodbye.

The case became interesting … Hayedeh and I were not sure what to do. I saw her the next day. I went to her. I did not know what to do. At the time, I had established friendly relations with one of the guards in Aminabad. I went to him and told him the whole story … And I stressed that if it was true, we were both responsible. He promised to follow it up.

We would wrap up shooting in Aminabad the following day. I told him we would not be returning to Aminabad from the day after. He gave me his number to call and get the updates…

He called me a few days later. I was truly anxious. He said: "I've investigated the case. That lady is telling the truth."

I was overjoyed.

He said: "I'll bar those "non-relative" relatives from leaving the country." He called again a few days later to say that he had taken the lady home.

To this day, I keep thinking that perhaps there are other patients in Aminabad who may never have had the chance to speak before their injection.

Flashback

I was a sixth former. I had just made it to the "Part" theatre group headed by my brother Davoud. I was studying at Shahid Alavi High School in Mashhad and was also active at the centre for religious debate and criticism which was run by Seyed Hassan Abtahi and Shahid Hasheminejad. I also worked at the Etelaat newspaper as a reporter and drew caricatures too.

The editor-in-chief of Etelaat newspaper in Mashhad [provincial capital of Khorasan], whose name I do not recall but remember him well, was a good person. One day, he asked me for a photograph so that he could introduce me as a young artist from Khorasan in northeastern Iran. I grew wings of happiness.

I went to the Muguet Studio, where Mostafa worked. I cannot remember his surname. I asked him to take an artistic photo of me; one of those portraits where one side of the face is in the shadows; and he did. I was really happy with my picture and I handed it in. The following week, in the Khorasan page of the Etelaat newspaper, about seven or eight lines had been printed in a column under the same picture. The title read: "A Young Artist from Khorasan". They had written about me as young stage actor, caricaturist, and reporter. But because my picture had been reduced in size and half of my face was in dark, it had turned out to be a disaster. I was barely visible.

Around the same time, the hajis and local religious people had gone to Saheb Alzaman Mosque and shown my picture to Haji

Abtahi. By pointing out my black lips in the picture, they had argued that Reza is hooked on heroin. They were not concerned about my own lips which were not black.

Afternoon – Outdoors – Foothill College

We had been to see a dance performance by Shahrokh Moshkin Ghalam with Hayedeh, Sadir, Sepideh Khosrojah, and Hamid Ehya.

1. We were climbing up the outer staircase which had numerous steps. The topic of discussion was whether anyone could climb this many stairs and smoke too? I saw a tall woman climbing down while smoking. I pointed her out as my witness. Sepideh said: "She's climbing down; it's the climbing up which counts." As we reached each other, she turned out to be Sepideh's friend. She came to us, said hello, and introduced herself. I also introduced myself. She said: "You don't need an introduction. I'm one of your fans." I also introduced my wife. She was her namesake. Another group of Iranian ladies who had also come to watch the programme were climbing up the stairs until they reached us. One of them said hello and I answered back, but she said: "Good grief, no one answers back." Apparently, they all had thought she had said hello to the next person; so when they heard her complain, they all said hello simultaneously to show that we are wonderful people.

2. We were waiting outside the hall. Some people would recognise me and come and say hello. Of course, they were all unhappy about the political situation in Iran and kept asking about it. But what they asked had a predictable answer, which they expected. The chances of the US attacking Iran was the topic of the day and they were all anxious. They were surprised by Hayedeh's and my carefree attitude and asked how do you put up with it? And I'd reply: "By the way, how do you put up with this place?"

3. One of the ladies talking to me pointed to one direction and said: "That old actor is here too. I looked and saw Behrouz Vosoughi. I made my excuses to that lady and went to talk with Behrouz. He saw me too and came towards me. We said a warm hello and hugged. I had always admired him. I liked him. I tell him that every time I see him; and I told him again this time. He introduced me to his wife. I'd never seen her before. She was a distinguished lady.

Flashback

One day, the late Fardin, may he rest in peace, told me: "I'm an actor, but I don't act. I'm like a fish out of water." That fish continued to jump up and fall back down; he tried so hard; so much so that that he finally died outside the bowl.

The Present Time

Inside the hall, before the show, Ms Homa Sarshar came to the podium and introduced the programme. Then, she proceeded to introduce every actor in the hall: Sadr-e-Din Elahi, Behrouz Vosoughi … and a few others that I did not know. They would stand up and the audience would applaud and shout-out. In the end, after many pleasantries and compliments, she said that a performer had come from Iran and announced my name. I still had Behrouz on my mind.

Hamid told me: "Get up, come on get up." I stood up, the audience clapped and screamed, and I sat down. But I still had Behrouz on the mind.

Flashback

The late Fardin had a screenplay on Sheikh Sanan which was

never made into a movie. He endured his days out of water with mysticism. Behrouz, too, endured with mysticism alongside his wife.

4. Hayedeh, the same tall lady who was my wife's namesake, came and asked: "What do you think about those of us who live abroad?"

"Do I look like I can think?"

She was speechless and confused. When she relaxed, we laughed and I said: "What am I supposed to think?"

Many Iranians who live abroad feel guilty. Many are in two minds about it. They miss Iran when they are abroad, and they miss abroad when they are in Iran.

I said: "I'd rather not be in your shoes."

"We're all born on this planet." My wife said.

5. An elderly couple came towards me, happy that they had spotted me. The man said: "Did we watch your movie last night?"

"I'm sorry I wasn't at your place to know which movie you watched."

"I mean we watched your movie last night." He said.

6. After the programme, a young girl asked for a picture, and with the first picture, a wave of requests followed. It is always the same. It seems that many people want to take a picture or get an autograph, but they won't. I do not know why? When the first autograph is given or the first picture is taken, others follow. It is as if they are waiting for the first person. Anyway, we started taking pictures. The most interesting was an elderly lady who was walking with a stick. She wanted to take a picture with me and her daughter. When we posed and were ready, she suddenly remembered that she was holding a walking stick. She did not want to be in the picture with a stick.

That is what many are like. They do not wish their disabilities and shortcomings to be eternelised in pictures. This is the magic of photographs. She was looking for someone or some place to get rid of the walking stick for a brief moment. I took it and said: "Please allow me to hold it."

I stood in the middle with a walking stick and the two ladies by either side without a stick. A souvenir photo was taken.

P.S. A few ladies saw me the following year in Iran and said I was in a photograph, holding their aunt's walking stick. They had seen the photo.

Day – Indoors – Macy's

We were walking along with Hayedeh and shopping. A couple of salespeople showed us to each other. I did not think they knew I was an actor, because I was in the US, not Iran. I saw the salespeople make another move or two. They were looking at me. It made me suspicious. I thought to myself what could have happened? Do I look like a runaway? Aha … a terrorist …? Until one of them approached me and asked in Persian: "Are you an actor?"

I said: "Yes, why?"

She screamed and the others ran too. They were all Iranians. I had heard that many Iranians work at Macy's, but had never seen it for myself. One of them said shyly: "When I saw you, I thought you were an actor from Pakistan. I said to my friend I think that gentleman is a Pakistanis actor, but his wife is American! But my friend said you were Iranian, and another friend told us who you were. I'm sorry." They all were. Then we saw a few other Iranians who were salespeople. But we could not shop there anymore, because we wanted to buy clothes that were on sale and we were too embarrassed to go look at those.

Day – Outdoors – Mashhad

For his film "The Red Ribbon", Mehrdad Mirkiani had cropped my hair and thinned my beard. I looked like an Afghan. I had to play the role of "Jomeh". I had gone to Mashhad for my father's commemoration ceremony on the fortieth day of this death. At his graveside, I was standing really close to my late mother, almost clinging to her. My mother nudged me and said quietly: "Move over; people will think who's this clinging to this woman."

After the ceremony, we were entertaining those who had attended at the Yas restaurant in Mashhad. My brother Vahid and I were standing by the door welcoming people. A young lad ran breathless, looking for someone. He ignored me and went straight to Vahid, asking: "Is Reza Kianian here? I heard he's in Mashhad. They said he was here."

Vahid asked: "What do you want with him?"

He said: "I want to be an actor. I've brought my pictures."

Vahid said: "OK. Give them to me. I'll pass them on to him!"

He gave the pictures to Vahid feeling helpless, and stressed: "You won't forget?"

Vahid said: "Sure", and gave me the photos right in front of him, adding: "Hold on to these."

"Sure." I said.

The boy looked at me, dilly-dallied a bit, and told Vahid: "Can you hold on to them? He might lose them."

He was right. I did lose them.

Day – Outdoors – Qeshm

One day, the IRGC commanders came to "The Red Ribbon"

shooting scene to see Hatamikia, Parviz Parastui, and myself.

Hatamikia and Parviz were standing next to each other when they arrived. I could see them exchanging pleasantries from a distance. It seems they had enquired about me, because Hatamikai looked around for a while until he spotted me and signalled that I should join them.

The tea person for the crew was taking them tea. I took the tray from him, told him he was relieved of duty, and took the tray to them. They took their tea. I just stood there. Hatamikia and Parviz were laughing and the commanders felt unease at my presence. They must have been thinking what a brazen Afghan! Finally, Hatamikia introduced me. They were now happy that I was there.

Day – Indoors – Manouchehr Shāhsavāri's Office

Abolhasan Davoudi wanted to make the "Rain Man". He phoned Parviz and I in Qeshm when we were shooting "The Red Ribbon" and sent the screenplay so we would not sign another contract after that.

We made an appointment when we went back to Tehran. I went to Manouchehr's office. He was shocked to see me; I did not know why.

... Finally, he said: "What happened to your hair?"

"I cropped it for 'The Red Ribbon'." I said.

"I wanted your long hair. I wanted you to put your fingers through it every now and then. No can do without hair." He replied.

Day – Outdoors – Around Khorramabad

We were filming outside one of Iran's central cities. All the actors were locals. The only non-locals were me, the cameraman, and the photographer.

In one of the scenes, I had to sit in front of the bicycle of one of the locals and he was supposed to take me across the mountains, plains, and river… The frames were supposed to dissolve from one to the next. We shot the scenes in the plains and river and arrived at the mountains.

The director was sitting on the opposite hill with the cameraman. He shouted at the robust local actor from there and said: "Get off the bike and start climbing." I sent a message to the director that if he climbed with the bicycle on his shoulders, it might look nicer. The director agreed and shouted again from the same hill: "Put the bike on your shoulders and climb."

The robust local actor shouted back: "With Kianian?"

Day – Indoors – Hospital

In "My Mother Gisoo" by Siamak Shayeghi, there is a scene in which I am hospitalised. My leg is in a cast and I'm sleeping on the bed under a blanket. Actress Yasaman Maleknasr is supposed to come and visit me and we are going to have a love dialogue.

It was an old hospital near the railway station downtown. It was summer and hot. The room was filled with projectors which added to the heat by manifold. The door and windows were shut to keep the noise out for the sound recording. It was so hot that Hamid Hamzeh, the makeup artist, kept wiping the sweat off my face every two minutes and powdered it to stop it from shining.

The scenes preceding the one with Maleknasr lasted until one in the afternoon. The film programmer, Shahram Shah-Hosseini, stopped the filming and said let's go to lunch. It was decided to shoot the romantic scene after lunch. Like most days on the set of most movies, lunch that day was minced meat kebabs and rice!

We had lunch and a rest, and returned to the set feeling heavy with sleep. My makeup was renewed. I put the cast on my leg and slept under the blanket. It was not hot, it was burning. Until everything was ready and Bahram Badakhshani's camera clicked, it was already three in the afternoon…

I beg you to put yourself in my shoes. I was picked up at five in the morning. At six o'clock I was having makeup put on. Then I got dressed. I had breakfast at seven thirty and then started the scene. And I was still in that same room. After all that heat, which had baked me into a mature man, and after the kebab and rice had bloated my stomach … now I had to utter love words and, especially, cast romantic looks!

Night – Indoors – Mansion

On one of the night shifts, when filming "A House Built on Water" by Bahman Farmanara in Dr Sepidbakht's house at one in the morning, we had to shoot a scene in which I had to cry in front of a large painting by Mostafa Dashti before the camera pulled back. To do the scene, the lighting in the entire hallway and large sitting room had to be sorted out. It took a couple of hours.

Little by little, the dust of sleep spread over our eyes. When the scene was ready, the entire house was at once filled with very loud Flamenco music. We were all wide awake now. Bahman Farmanara started dancing with his chubby figure and called me to dance too. I, too, had put on weight for the film and was looking chubby. I joined Bahman Farmanara and we danced stomach to stomach. Everyone was wide awake, energetic, and ready to go.

Filming began and one of the saddest, most effective scenes was shot.

Flashback

In the same movie, I had withdrawn into my shell and getting ready to shoot another sad, emotional scene, when Farmanara came and whispered a really funny joke in my ear. We burst out laughing. Then I told him: "I was getting into the mindset of a sad scene. Why did you mess up my mood?"

He said: "You're supposed to be an actor. So act."

Day – Night – Indoors

It was Ramadan. A young man phoned and, after many apologies and words of respect, he said: "We would like to invite you to come to our mission on the night of Ahya vigil on the 23rd and talk for us!"

I said: "Don't you think you've got the wrong person? It's customary on these nights to invite a cleric."

He said: "We're a special mission."

"My dear man, I'm no speech maker, especially not a religious one."

"Yes Sir. We know you. That's why we're inviting you."

I became suspicious, and said: "At any rate, this is not what I do. On these nights, I'm a listener myself. I do apologise; may God give you what you're seeking elsewhere."

He insisted. He kept on insisting.

"Look my brother, I don't know you. Who are you?" I asked.

"We're a group of young men. We've been running this religious mission for ten years now, and…"

He gave some more explanations and promised to send some documents on their mission within the next couple of days.

Two days later, I received a package at home, containing photos, a brochure, and a text introducing them. They were really up-to-date. It looked like what I had wished for in the old days when I was active at the centre for religious debate and criticism in Mashhad. I became interested.

He phoned later to ask: "Did you see the photos? Did you read the text?"

"I did and I'm interested. I'll come to your mission on the Ahya vigil, but I won't deliver a speech. I'll come to see you and spend Ahya with you." And I said goodbye.

He phoned again the following day to say please say a few words when you come.

"I'll decide when I get there."

At first, their ceremony was supposed to be held at Enghelab Cultural Centre; then, the venue was changed to the artistic activities hall of the Institute for the Intellectual Development of Children and Young Adults. I am still not accustomed to sitting on chairs on Ahya night. I think one must sit on the floor. But this was a cinema and theatre hall. We had to sit on chairs!

I went to Vesal Street at ten o'clock at night. The place was packed. There was nowhere to park on either side of the street. The space on both sides of the traffic island was also full. As luck would have it, I finally found somewhere to park the car. I could not believe that the mission had this many supporters. I went to the hall. Other people were walking in the same direction as me. They were mostly young, like all the people we see on the street. The same boys and girls we see on a daily basis.

When we walked in, well-dressed young people ushered the people to their seats. One of them saw me and came over. He welcomed and guided me. A few people were also taking photos. He took me inside the hall which was full of people. He sat me down in the darkness of the hall. One or two people sitting in the same row said hello, but I was unable to see them as my eyes were still not used to the dark. I also said hello. The Jawshan Kabir prayer was being read. It was projected on the cinema screen with a Persian translation and read by a voice. Later, I saw a young man reading it on the stage. When my eyes became used to the dark, I noticed a number of directors from the Ministry of Culture and Islamic Guidance, during the time of Dr Masjed- Jamei, and a few directors of the Institute for the Intellectual Development of Children and Young Adults. They were the ones who had said hello. We exchanged pleasantries and I started listening to the prayer again.

A few of the young TV presenters were there. One of them was reading the Jawshan Kabir prayer.

The prayer finished around a quarter to eleven. The lights came on in the hall and it was announced in the loudspeakers that refreshments were being served outside the hall. At this point, Dr Masjed-Jamei also arrived. After exchanging greetings with me and his directors, he said his wife and children were attendees of the mission.

Some of the young people came and guided us to the refreshments table. We sat down with the Minister of Guidance, his deputies, and the director of the Institute. We had zulbia-bamieh sweets with tea and chatted.

It was finally announced in the loudspeakers that we should return to the hall. One of them told me: "Once the guests are settled, we will invite you to come and say a few words."

I felt at ease with them now. I sat down. Everyone did. The young TV presenter, Jalilvand, started the programme. He greeted the audience, said the usual spiel with much panegyrics. Eventually, he asked me to go on stage. As a rule, going on stage must be run-of-the-mill for me. But to this day, it is not; even when I am doing a play; even when I am giving or getting a prize. My heart begins to race as I walk up the stage and all the weight of the world is on my shoulders. I forget everything. This is how I felt when they called my name. But I must also add that as I walk on stage, it is as if I have walked into a new world. A world with its own rules. Everything calms down. I never prepare a speech, because I have the experience. I will say something different when I get there. Except for my scripts which I practice over and over again.

I walked on the stage with a blank mind. I enjoy the anxiety.

I knew Jalilvand from before. We said hello on the stage. He asked me questions relevant to that night and I gave him some answers when, all of a sudden, something flooded my mind. I hesitated, tasted it. I could not resist pouring it out. I was looking at the audience in their seats. All eyes were on me. On this night, which is most probably the Night of Decree, the doors of the heavens are open and the whole world welcomes you. I turned to Jalilvand and said: "If you'll allow me, I'd like to move on from pleasantries and say something."

I said: These are the Ahya nights; the nights to come alive, to be revived. There is no need to cry. These are happy nights. My artistic ancestors also came to life in my mind. They came on stage with me. They are right here. My artistic ancestors are actors, musicians, and singers. Do you know what they were called up to seventy or eighty years ago? Minstrels, meaning hired musicians. The meaning of the word is good, even suitable for tonight, because Ahya is a happy occasion. But the accepted meaning was different. It was jocular, light, cheap and disrespectful. This is how your ancestors saw my ancestors. I don't know how they would have felt had they known that, one day, their great grandchildren would invite the great grandchildren of hired musicians for this dear, respectful Night of Decree and even ask them to deliver a speech on the pulpit. They poured the water of repentance on the heads of hired musicians before they were allowed into these ceremonies. Your ancestors only invited mine to weddings and circumcision celebrations to bring them joy and happiness. They were rejected and avoided the next day. They were prohibited. A hired musician was unlawful, disallowed. The remains of this way of thinking continue to linger on.

Your ancestors would not allow the corpses of my ancestors to be buried in Muslim cemeteries, in case their torment of the grave was passed on to them; in case the due blessings of their dead were denied them because of my ancestors. This is why the bodies of my ancestors were buried away from them, in graveyards reserved for the infidel.

I am amazed that on this night, which is worth a thousand nights, you have invited a hired musician and actor to speak for you, the faithful! Perhaps it is a premiere. On this Night of Decree, I would like to ask you to say a prayer for my ancestors on behalf of your ancestors.

Flashback

In elementary school, when I was eight or nine, there was a busker in the city of Mashhad called "Jiki-Jiki Naneh Khanoum"[2]. Not that this was his name, but a fictitious name the people knew him by. He was a tall, skinny man with straight hair. His complexion was black-a-vised and he wore rags for clothes. Perhaps he was from Southern Khorasan.

He had a dotar and a small wooden board on which a goat puppet called "Bozi" shook its joints. He would tie a piece of string around one of the fingers on his right hand; the same hand he used to play the strings of his dotar. The other end of the string was connected to Bozi on the wooden board. When he played, the string was pulled and the goat dangled around as if dancing to the tune of the dotar. He sang a singsong with the tune of the dotar, with the refrain "Jiki-Jiki Naneh Khanoum". His tired, raspy voice is still engraved on my mind.

Occasionally, I would see him when I went to Ark Street in Mashhad. I'd ask my father to wait, to stay where he was so that I could watch him. He was a busker and given a ha'penny or two if he was in luck. I'd also ask my father to give him some money.

---

2 Jiki-Jiki Grandma

People used to say he is an addict; that he has smoked so much opium that it did not drug him anymore; that he would go to "Kouh Sangi" stony mountain and stick his hand in a snake hole to get a buzz from the sting. They said the snake would then die, because there was so much poison in Jiki-Jiki Naneh Khanoum's body that it would poison the snake. Everybody stayed away. When he died, the Council was supposed to take his body to "Golshour" graveyard on the outskirts of town. A high-ranking colonel had also died at the same time as him. He was going to be buried in the courtyard of Imam Reza's shrine. When someone pulled the shroud from the late colonel's face for his family to say their last goodbyes at the graveside, everyone saw that Jiki-Jiki Naneh Khanoum was lying in the grave at the courtyard of Imam Reza's shrine instead of the colonel whose body had been mistakenly taken to Golshour. When a body is placed in a grave, no one is allowed to take it out and transfer it to another grave.

Jiki-Jiki Naneh Khanoum stayed in the courtyard of Imam Reza's shrine, which is said to be a piece of heaven, under the protection of the Eighth Imam forever.

Night – Indoors – Khaniabad Cultural Centre Theatre Stage

I spent my Sundays sitting at the foot of the late Dulabi's pulpit and listened. A member of the religious missions who attended the place asked me to go to Khaniabad on the night of Hazrat Masoumeh Zahra's (SA) birthday. He said: "We celebrate there every year. Why don't you come too and go on stage for a few minutes so that the kids on the outskirts of town can see you close-up too."

On the due date, I went there at five o'clock. It was packed. The feast was on with illuminations. There was cream cakes and sherbet. I went backstage. The person who had invited me was also the presenter. He sat me down to wait for my turn. Eventually, he came and said: "Get ready; you're on in a few minutes."

A few minutes later, I could hear him saying on stage to the people: "One of the actors of cinema and television that you all know - etc, etc - is here tonight. I invite him to come on stage now: Reza Kianian!"

I walked on the stage. People clapped and whistled and laughed. They were happy. I congratulated them on the occasion of Eid. I said my mother's name is Zahra. I am thinking of her today. I said I am happy to be here with you today…

The presenter asked me a few questions, like how many children do you have? What's your son's name? And so on. I answered patiently and made a few jokes to make people laugh, which they did. When his questions were over and it was time to say goodbye, he said: "And this is another gift of the Islamic Revolution to guide these immoral actors who sinned before the revolution towards Islam so that they come among us to celebrate the birthday of Hazrat Zahra (SA)!

Night – Indoors – Mashhad Airport

1. We were waiting to go to the transit lounge with Azadeh Akhlaghi. The other passengers came to take pictures with me and get autographs. These days, everyone has mobiles which double up as cameras. Sometimes people get carried away and think that if they do not get my autograph or take a picture with me, they have missed an important occasion. That night was one of those nights. Everyone came. Little by little, I was getting tired and praying that the loudspeaker would announce that the passengers on our flight should go to the transit lounge. It was amid my exhaustion and prayers that I heard my name being announced on the PA system to go to information. It was an added problem. I kept thinking what could have happened, what was the problem that they were calling me? Because we are used to expecting bad news all the time. We always have to prove our innocence.

I made my apologies to a few people who were waiting for a photo and autograph and went to the information desk. When I arrived there, the two ladies behind the desk smiled sweetly when they saw me, and said: "Sorry, we saw you were here, but couldn't leave our desk to come and see you. So we called for you to come here. How are you?"

2. Same night, same place

One of the shopkeepers at the airport in those shops that sell the gifts and souvenirs of Mashhad, came up to me, said hello, and gave me his notebook to sign. I signed it and was about to go, when he said: "Excuse me, I don't have a camera on me right this minute. But please don't be upset. You wait here and I'll find one in two shakes of a lamb's tail to take a photo of us both."

3. Same night, transit lounge

There was signing and taking photos in the transit lounge too. For instance, a lady whose infant was sleeping woke her up and handed her to me, pleading. As she cooed her baby, she took a selfie of us all.

Two Isfahani girls also came and said although they had taken a picture with me in Isfahan, they still wanted another one. They took their photo, gave me some gum, and left. They did not hesitate to think whether I wanted gum or not. A few moments later, one of them turned around and said: "By the way, that jacket you're wearing really suits you! But don't wear it, because the Mashhadis have an evil eye and, God forbid, will harm you!

Day – Indoors – Orly Airport, Paris

We were walking out of Orly Airport together with Mohammad Tahtkeshian, Reza Attaran, and Mr Mousavi and his wife.

An elderly Iranian lady discovered me. She came up to me and pointed out a thirty-year-old lady who was holding a child, saying: "This is my daughter. She's loved you ever since she was a child." I said hello to her and we exchanged pleasantries. I was in a rush to go because the others were waiting for me. After saying goodbye, I added: "Your son – the child she was holding in her arms – looks very much like me when I was a child.

The young lady gave out a muted gasp and gave her a son a juicy kiss on the cheek!

Day – Indoors – Pilot's Cabin, Iran Air

On many flights, especially long-haul flights, the crew are very kind to me and invite me into the pilot's cabin.

1. We were on a flight to Paris when the pilot invited me into his cabin.

   I was talking to him and his assistant as I looked out of the cockpit windshield. We were flying over the clouds which were scattered, displaying the snow-capped mountains of Germany and its fields. I asked the pilot: "You mostly watch the earth from the sky; does this angle affect you in any way?"

   He said: "Very … very."

   I said: "Do you mind explaining?"

   He said: "It makes life's problems shrink for me. I don't get too involved in them and just skip over them. I tell my wife too, but she doesn't see it my way. She gets involved."

2. I was flying to Iran from Holland the following year, again on Iran Air, and again I was a guest of the pilot's cabin. I told him what the previous pilot has said to me.

He said: "What difference does it make whether you're up here or down there? When we're up here, we're always thinking about controlling the airplane and all these buttons.

And when we're on the ground, we get caught up in all the difficulties down there.

What's important is to live no matter where you are and not get taken up by routine. You won't get anywhere by chilla-nashini and sitting in a corner. You will, but you won't reach your zenith. Everything changes when you join the crowds. If you're a man! be with the people and reach your zenith...

Ascetics sit in a corner in seclusion.

It is not clear if they can feel the same when they join the people again.

I said: "I like your outlook. Two years ago, someone had returned from India and was telling me in amazement that he had seen an ascetic who submerged himself in the river in the morning, and emerged again at sundown. I was not surprised and told him a frog can do that too. Those who walk on water don't surprise me either, because mosquitos can do that too. The tough, amazing task for a person is to live with the people and be a good person; to respect everyone and not violate their rights.

"So you see, it's not important whether we're on the clouds or under the clouds. It's important to be a good human being." He said.

Day – Indoors – Airplane

I was flying to Isfahan. I was alone. I was going to attend an accreditation ceremony for my brother Davoud. He was going to be honoured at the Children and Youth Theater Festival. They had asked me to say a few words about him and present him with the award.

The employee who issued my boarding pass kindly gave me the window seat. She did not know that I preferred the aisle seat. I boarded the plane. When I found my seat, I saw that a young girl was in the window seat, staring outside. She did not notice me, or pretended not to notice me. It was a small plane; one of those with rows of two seats on one side, and rows of three seats on the other.

I was in no mood to argue and was only too happy to be in the aisle seat. I started reading a book. I continued to read until we reached Isfahan. When I wanted to look out of the window, I could see that the girl avoided my look. To make her feel comfortable, I stopped looking out.

We landed at Isfahan airport. As the plane was taxiing, the girl said to me: "I'm sorry Mr Kianian, would you mind if I ask you a personal question?"

I said: "You can ask; I may answer."

"Don't you have to say hello to your fellow traveller when you get on the plane?" She said.

"Am I the one who was supposed to say hello?"

"You're a man. You're supposed to say hello to women."

"But when men just say hello to women they don't know, they take it the wrong way."

"How?"

"The way you're thinking now."

She was a bit embarrassed. She went quiet. The plane had come to a stop. I picked up my bag and left.

Night – Indoors - The Children and Youth Festival Closing Ceremony

There were many people at the ceremony. Around thirty or forty children in folk costume were on stage, and about the same number were seated in the centre of the hall. The guests were there too, from theatre actors to authorities of the Ministry of Islamic Guidance, law enforcement, MPs, and authorities of the city of Isfahan.

The presenter was someone from a children's programme on television. According to his routine, he talked less and mostly sang rhythmic songs while asking everyone to clap their hands. The children clapped, but the ministry and city officials sat quietly. We also sat quietly and watched, but the presenter insisted that we clap and accompany him! Eventually, he turned to me from the stage and said: "Mr Reza, why won't you join in? Have you forgotten your childhood?"

I signalled to say you carry on with your job.

It was then my turn to go on stage to pay tribute to my brother Davoud and present him with his award.

I said hello to everyone, and started: "An important lesson taught to me and the members of the theatre group by Davoud, which has always guided me to this day, is not to beg the audience to be on my side. I should convince them to join me with my acting; to like and respect me. Davoud has written about thirty plays for children and young adults, a few have which have had record-breaking performances nationwide. He also has a number of research books on the theatre for children and young adults which are rather original in their kind. He voices his own singular opinion on the theatre for children and young adults, which can be discussed at the global level … and he continues to study and research. All countries progress through research. Research produces science, research guides, and research shows the way and brings mastery."

I asked the authorities responsible for the national theatre why the Center for the Performing Arts did not have a research centre. And I added that Davoud Kianian will be presented with this award tonight, but will continue to stay as home as from tomorrow night when he should be at the Research Institute of Theater for Children and Adolescents. Davoud accepted his award amid the applause of the audience. When I left the stage, everyone from the Artistic Deputy of the Ministry of Guidance to MPs all said how right I was. They said we will invite you to start up a research centre when we return to Tehran. But there is no news yet!

Night – Outdoors – Tehran

There is a kebab shop at the top of our alley. I was returning home with Davoud Amiri. I was about to turn into our alley when I came across a Hillman Paykan car parked sideways across the street at the top of the alley and I had to use my acrobatic talents to drive into the alley. As I was busy with my acrobatics, I noticed someone was leaning on the back of the car and smoking.

I pulled down the window and pointedd at the Hillman Paykan: "Is this your car?" He said: "Aha!" As if he was not parked in the middle of the junction.

"Nice job parking." I said.

"I've ordered kebabs!" He replied.

Day – Indoors – Hospital

Davoud Mousayi had been hospitalised. I phoned him to see how he was. Marjanbanou said: "He's still in the operating theatre at Arad Hospital."

I went to visit him a couple of hours later. But I went to Mehran Hospital insteas, which was the wrong place. I finally found a parking space at great pain by driving around a few times. I rushed into the hospital and walked into the emergency. As I was walking through the emergency corridor to reach the lobby, I noticed about seven or eight people standing in the corridor and crying. They included three women between thirty and forty, two or three young girls, an elderly lady on a wheelchair, and two men who were consoling the ladies. It was evident that their patient has passed away.

One of the women was crying and sobbing really hard. One of the men said: "He's in a better place now."

The sobbing woman kept repeating: "He's in a better place; he's in a better place."

I was really touched and walked past them quietly. As soon as I had stepped away from them, I heard the woman say: "He's in a better place now, sob, sob … But this is Mr Kianian; he's in a better place now."

I turned around and gave them my condolences.

Still sobbing, the woman said: "How … are you?"

I said: "I'm well, thank you."

The woman continued: "Any … new … works?"

The girls said hello shyly and coquettishly.

The men came up and shook hands.

I saw the elderly lady who was asking who is this by moving her eyes and eyebrows.

One of the girls whispered some explanations into her ear. The elderly lady shook her head to say she had understood and then scanned me from head to toe with her curious eyes brimming with tears.

Day – Night – Indoors – Outdoors – Mecca

1. We were on pilgrimage to Mecca with film and TV people Kamal Tabrizi, Hassan Pourshirazi, Uncle Pourang,[3] Cyrus Moghaddam, and others in the group which was supervised by Mr Norouzbeigi. The other pilgrims in the group were ordinary citizens.

   Our fellow pilgrims were surprised to see us. Other Iranians in other pilgrimage groups who saw us in Mecca and Medina were also surprised, and asked: "You come to Mecca too?" Or they would say: "You are so lucky."

---
3 Presenter of children's programme (Amou Pourang)

It was as if we were new converts to Islam. They would ask us to pray for them.

Hired musicians and Mecca!?

2. We had gone to pick up a friend with Kamal Tabrizi. They were saying the last part of their prayer in congregation. Afterwards, he came to us and dragged us to show to their chaplain. The chaplain recognised me, said hello, and added: "Mashaallah, how illuminated you look."

I said: "Haji, we were illuminated before."

He said: "I mean your beard."

I said: "The heart must be illuminated. You can be ostentatious with a beard too, but not in the heart."

He said: "You've been honoured to visit Mecca."

I said: "Haji, every time we play a part in a movie, series, or play, it is in fact like visiting Mecca for us."

3. When Iranians saw us, they were both surprised and happy to get an autograph or take a picture. It is an interesting contradiction. They like us on the one hand, and we are hired musicians on the other.

Uncle Pourang had the most fans. They wanted a selfie with him to take back to their children.

Next, it was Hassan Pourshirazi. The series "Narges" had just finished being aired and everyone wanted to know about the behind the scenes events. They called him by his character's name "Shokat".

And I was last. I had my own special fans. There was always a crowd waiting outside the hotel or our tents in Mina and Arafat.

4. There was a religious eulogist in our group who had been honoured to come with his family. He was on good terms with us. He would say: "Artists have pure hearts." He had a camera and filmed us to take back to his kith and kin.

One afternoon, we were alone in a corner, me and him. He was saying that he was the eulogist for Imam Hossein. He said both him and his family were the waqf of Imam Hossein.

I asked him: "You who have dedicated your life to eulogising Imam Hossein, do you know anything more about him apart from the last month of his life?

He was a fair man. He remained silent.

I asked: "For how long was he an Imam? What did he do in those years? What kind of Imam was he? How did he get to Mecca? Why did he leave his hajj unfinished? I don't know. But you should."

He remained silent … And finally said: "You're right. I know nothing. I was destined to find out in Mecca that I know nothing. When I go back to Iran, I will certainly read about it."

5. When we were visiting the Quba Mosque in Medina, I saw a group of African men and women gathered in its courtyard. Someone, perhaps their guide, was talking to them. Maybe he was preparing them to go and visit the mosque as pilgrims. I had a camera and wanted to take their picture. I asked an elderly lady who was looking at me: "Can I take a picture." She shook her head Yes. I had taken a few pictures when they started towards the mosque. They would sing "Ya Mohammad (PBUH)" in a jazz rhythm, dance, and go towards the mosque. I was so taken by their singing and dancing that I totally forgot to take more pictures.

A few days later, I saw the same old lady amid the crowd as I was circling the Kabaa. She was dancing and chanting "Ya Allah" and circling the Kabaa to the same rhythm. She saw me, smiled, and disappeared in the crowd.

6. The crew from one of our TV networks who were filming a report saw me. The reporter came up to me and asked: "Do we have your permission for an interview."

I said: "What about?"

He said: "About how you're doing in Mecca."

I said: "Do you give interviews about your private life, say your bedroom?"

He said: "What's it got to do with that?"

I said: "In the bedroom, there are two people and God. This is even more private, because there's one person and God."

Day – Outdoors – Tehran

We were working on Farzad Motamen's film "The Voices". It was ten in the morning; a street off Jamalzadeh Avenue. I had to stand in the street and ring Atila Pesyani's door bell. All throughout the takes, housemakers who were going to do their shopping or were on their way back home would come and say hello when they saw me. Some invited me to tea. For instance, one woman said: "We've just moved to this area today. I'll take seeing you as a good omen; and she insisted that I pay them a visit after filming. Others who see me walk up to me, and others behave as if they have not seen me, or that seeing me is not important to them, but they still peep at me from the corner of their eye. Two of these ladies were returning home with their shopping. One of them saw me and nudged the other woman in the side. Then, she pointed at me; the other woman also saw and recognised me, but both pretended not to have seen me!

They talked and walked towards us. It was obvious that they were talking about me. When they walked past me, I heard one of them say: "It's either a movie or a CD!"

Night – Outdoors – Isfahan

This sort of thing happens often. When I am passing through some place and someone is coming towards me, they signal to their friend to show me to them too. By the time the other person has noticed, I've already walked past and they have missed me. To see me without me noticing, they turn around, run past me, and stop and look at the window of a shop for instance; to pretend that they've run to look at the shop. Under this pretext, they look around again, see me, and feel reassured.

Night – Outdoors – Isfahan

This sort of thing happens often. When I am passing through some place and someone is coming towards me, they signal to their friend to show me to them too. By the time the other person has noticed, I've already walked past and they have missed me. To see me without me noticing, they turn around, run past me, and stop and look at the window of a shop for instance; to pretend that they've run to look at the shop. Under this pretext, they look around again, see me, and feel reassured.

If I am not in a rush, I play a game with my passing visitors. Something similar happened in Isfahan once. The person walked past me and did not notice me at first. Then, he ran and stopped in front of a boutique. As soon as he turned around to look at me, I turned around too and my back was to him. He did not know what to do. He ran past me again. I turned around again and my back was to him again.

There was another game I played too. When the person runs and looks at the shop window, I say hello to them when they turn around. They are taken by surprise.

Then there are those who see me, walk up to me, and ask me: "Sorry, what was your name?"

"My name hasn't changed yet. It's still the same name."

Day – Indoors – Homa Hotel in Bandar Abbas

Years ago, I went to Bandar Abbas. I woke up early in the morning. I opened the curtains of my bedroom and let the light in. I was staying on the top floor. I was standing at the window and watching the streets.

A hairdresser's sign in one of the streets caught my eye. It said: "Afifeh [Virtuous] Women's Hairdresser. Former Malousak [Mignon]!"

Day – Outdoors – Plains of Kurdistan

We were on location in the plains of Kurdistan, near Kamyaran, to shoot "The Familiar Soil" by Bahman Farmanara.

In the scene, Babak Hamidian and I were supposed to walk past a few locals from the village while chatting. I had to say a few words to them, asking them how they were, in Kurdish naturally, because my character in the film was of Kurdish descent.

I had learned a couple of sentences from Ms Maryam Boubani and Farzin Sabouni, and I was going to repeat those.

As Mahmoud Kelari and Bahman Farmanara were getting ready, I was walking in the distance and practising the words and pronunciation of those two sentences: "Hal o bal" and "khaseh shakour". I was standing somewhere on a higher level. A shepherd and his herd of sheep unexpectedly appeared in front of me like the rising sun. The shepherd was surprised to see me in the plains.

He asked: "What're you doing here Mr Kianian?"

I said: "Hal o bal?" He was even more surprised to hear me speak Kurdish.

He said: "Thank you. What're you doing here?"

I said: "Khaseh shakour?"

He said: "Thank you. What're you doing here?"

I said: "Are you well and happy?"

He said: "Thank you. Goodbye."

He left like the sunset.

Day – Indoors – Jetway - London Airport

At the start of "A House Built on Water", there is a scene where I am sitting in the waiting room of a surgery. The woman I have taken home the night before is still there. She phones and starts to complain. The money I have left her is not enough. She wants me to tell my help to give her the bowl on the table of the hall with bird paintings on it instead of the missing money. The film was made in 2001 and screened later. And now, a few years later, I am walking in the jetway at London Heathrow to board the Iran Air flight. The Iranians who know me say hello. An energetic middle-aged lady runs in the crowd, says hello excitedly, and adds: "I'm so glad I've found you. I have a question to ask you that you must absolutely answer." I said: "Please let us board the plane first. There's plenty of time during the flight. I'm at your service." The plane took off and the initial refreshments were served. As I was exhausted by my ten-hour wait in Heathrow, I fell asleep. When I woke up, I decided to walk a few steps. A few people came to take pictures. Then, the crew took me to the back of the plane to take pictures with them. One of them said: "There's a lady who keeps looking for you, but you were asleep. And now she's asleep. It seems to be an urgent matter. Will you allow me to wake her up?"

I said: "OK."

The attendant woke her up and showed her to the back of the plane. It was the same lady. I saw her tidying herself up and walking towards us with a smile.

She had a camera on her. She reached us; said hello; hesitated; then asked in anger: "Why did you give that beautiful bowl with the bird paintings to that slut?"

I could tell from her accent that she was from Isfahan.

Night – Indoors – The Surgery of Dr Rezaei

There is a mole on the right hand side of my face. I am used to it. But another one gradually grew on the left hand side of my face as well. Just like the one on the right hand side.

Hayedeh is very sensitive towards this sort of thing. She insisted that I must show the new mole to the doctor. She does not feel comfortable with any doctors. One night, we eventually went to see Dr Rezaei at the Gharb Clinic whom she approves of. I got there late. I asked reception for a fee payment receipt. He said the doctor was not seeing patients anymore. But I had to see him … I went up without paying. He might see me yet.

A few patients were waiting for their turn. I told his secretary: "If at all possible, could you please ask the doctor to see me."

She had recognised me, but pretended not to.

She said: "The doctor will only see the patients who are waiting here. You must come another day." I insisted. She said: "You can wait if you like, but I know that he won't see anyone else."

Later, I found out that another person like me was there too and the secretary did not want to do me any favours in front of him.

At any rate, I kept waiting until the secretary's heart softened. She went in and came back out after a while, saying: "The doctor will see you."

The man who was waiting said: "But what about me? I was here first."

The secretary looked at me as if to say, you see; I have to send him in too now.

I also thanked her with my eyes and in words.

She said: "Please go downstairs and pay the fee." She said the same thing to the man who was waiting.

The man told me: "You can pay my fee too while you're down there."

And then gave me the money without waiting for an answer and sat back down.

I paid the two fees and returned upstairs. When I looked in my wallet, there was only a thousand tomans left!!

I was happy I had enough to pay the fee. I put some money in my wallet every once in a while. When I run out, I take some more from the house. But there are many times when I forget. At times, I have been shopping and realised I was short of money when I wanted to pay.

The secretary was on her way out. She told me: "You can go in after these patients." She said goodbye and left.

When the last patient came out, the man walked in with no mercy … He finally came out and left without saying goodbye.

I went in at last.

Dr Rezaei was a cool, but tired old man. I was seeing him for the first time. He told me to sit down. I sat down and told him about the mole.

He examined it and said: "It's nothing. It's an ordinary mole."

I said: "My wife is one of your patients. What shall I tell her? She might think I was never here."

He said: "I can remove it if you like."

I said: "Yes, if possible."

He stretched me out on the bed and removed it with his special instrument. I suddenly remembered that I had paid for an ordinary visit, but not to remove the mole. I had no money on me. I was looking for a solution in my mind when he said: "Get up."

I said: "Thank you for seeing me. How much do I owe you?"

He said: "Sit down."

I sat down.

"My secretary said you're an actor; is that right?"

"Yes."

"Are you in television as well?"

"Yes." I said.

He picked up pen and paper and said: "Tell me the names of the films and series you've been in."

I named them one by one and he wrote them down patiently.

When I was finished, he said: "I won't take any money from you for removing the mole, because I'll be happy at home with this piece of paper tonight."

I said: "How come?"

"My wife watches TV from dusk to dawn. When I get home tonight and tell her that I've met you, she'll be very happy and will treat me well. You can also tell your wife that I removed your mole and she'll treat you well too! Tit for tat."

Afternoon – Outdoors – Mirdamad

I was on my way to the Capital Computer Complex on Mirdamad Street with Davoud Amiri to buy an external hard drive. An elderly Arab woman was sitting in a corner, begging. She was wearing the traditional Arabic veil and the customary tattoos on her forehead and chin. When we walked past her, she said: "Well, Salman Khan is here too."

We walked past.

Davoud said: "Interesting, she knows Salman Khan too."

"Who's Salman Khan?" I said.

"You mean you don't know him? He's the famous Indian actor. She saw you, that's why she said Salman Khan is here too."

Day – Night – Indoors – Outdoors

When middle-aged or elderly ladies see and discover me, they tell each other: "Let me die for him, is it really him?"

They sound as if they are talking to a child, or about them! They speak about me at my age in a loving, motherly tone of voice.

When I say hello and I hope to God that they do not die, they say as if they have made another discovery: "May God strike me dead ... It's the same voice!"

Sometimes, young girls also say the "Let me die for him" expression.

I have asked myself on numerous occasions why ladies ask God for death so often.

Day – Indoors - Disciplinary Forces Bureau [of Properties]

I was at the Disciplinary Forces Bureau. As soon as the gang there saw me, they took me downstairs for tea and a chat.

We talked about everything. One of them sent someone to sort out my affairs. Another one who was on the radio non-stop told one of the officers who was chatting with me: "Tonight is the night," and gave him a password.

The officer looked distressed. He went quiet and looked sunken. He said: "Tonight, I must go to a brothel and bring everyone back here … Seven or eight girls and a madam in charge … Do you know how old the girls are? All under nineteen. They're like our own daughters. What difference does it make? He fell silent again.

We were all upset. We all went quiet.

He stood up to leave. "This is not a nice job. We're always in slough up to our knees."

Day – Night – Indoors – Outdoors – Isfahan

People have different reactions when they see me. Somemvb will walk up to me; others will wave from a distance. But when someone who recognised me in Isfahan came up to me and said: "So how do you like it that I recognised you?", his tone of voice made me feel as if I owed him something. The way he said it felt as if I had to reward and cheer him on. I thought to myself, well this is one way to react to. But on my next trips to Isfahan, I came across the same expression and tone of voice again: "So how do you like it that I recognised you?"

Day – Indoors – The Corridors of the Ministry of Islamic Guidance

When "Cinema is Cinema" was being readied for the film festival, Ziaeddin Dorri said to me: "The ministry has said that Kianian's name should only appear as an actor in the credits."

I was also the stage and costume designer.

"Why?" I asked.

"No idea; why don't you go and ask them."

I went to the Ministry of Culture and Islamic Guidance. I asked for the person in charge. I saw him in the corridor, exchanged greetings, and asked: "Why shouldn't my name appear as stage and costume designer in the credits?"

He said: "You don't need that. Your name will appear as the lead actor. Isn't that enough?"

"But I have both acted and designed."

"I know. But one must not seek too much name and fame."

"The credits are a movie's identity. This way, the identity will be distorted."

"Good grief, the main thing is the movie which will be seen by everyone!"

I realised that he would not come round no matter what I said. In those days, their policy was not to let anyone become a star; for nobody to make a name for themselves. I said: My dear brother, I have had different responsibilities in some of the movies and it has always appeared in the credits. This is the simplest right of someone who does something. I only did a couple of things in this movie.

I cannot recall how long I argued with him until the gentleman agreed and took back his orders!

Night – Indoors – Outdoors – House of Cinema

Hamid Samandarian was giving a speech at the House of Cinema. The Association of Actors had asked me to manage the session. It was a passionate speech. Afterwards, crowds of acting enthusiasts rushed towards Hamid Samandarian, myself, and the other actors who were there that night to listen to Samandarian speak. Everybody wants to be an actor, and they all ask the same question: "How do I become an actor?"

Often, I give them some explanations, but I was in a rush that night and had to dash. There are always others too, apart from the acting enthusiasts. Like a young photographer who insisted that I should pose for a portrait picture!

Or like someone else who, amid the crowd, kept insisting: "I only have the one question. I only need a second of your time; just one second. What is your philosophy on acting!?"

When I finally managed to exit and be saved, a shy young man – obviously from a small town – wanted to ask me a question in total embarrassment. I carried on walking, but then my heart went out to him and returned. I said: "Go on."

He said: "I'm from out of town. I want to become an actor. I've nowhere in Tehran. Which classes should I attend?" He asked me to help him. What kind of help could I give him?

I could not get his face out of my mind that night. What answer could I give him?

Day – Indoors – An Important Place

For the TV series "Mokhtarnameh" by Davood Mir-Bagheri, in which I was going to appear, I had fifteen makeup test sessions. I also had a few meetings with Abdollah Eskandari and Davood Mir-Bagheri.

In one of the sessions, Abdollah Eskandari concocted a fake nose for me; the same one which, subsequently, became crooked and remained on the face of Abdullah al-Zubayr, the ruler of Mecca. Kamran Khalaj, who is really fussy, stuck the nose on my face and put on latex glue all around it. Even in my nostrils. Latex is very elastic and stretches quite a bit.

To cut a long story short, Kamran himself cleaned my face and I went home.

The next day, I had a meeting with a few nice, clean people. I wanted to talk to them and ask them to sponsor the project.

I took a shower, put on my glad rags and went to the meeting. We talked at length. As we were getting to know each other, I felt that my right nostril was itching. Naturally, I scratched it. I felt a small, foreign object stuck in it. Naturally, I tried to clean it with a tissue. Trying to get that small, foreign object out was the end of my reputation. Hard as I tried to get it away from my nose, it was stuck and kept stretching. I let go of it in fear and shame. It bounced back to its place straight away. Everyone saw and I had no explanations.

It was a piece of the same latex which had not been removed.

Night – Outdoors – Imam Khomeini Airport

We were waiting outside the airport at the taxi rank with Gandom, Golnar, Sa'ad, Mostafa, Hayedeh, and Ali.

Two taxi drivers, each one with a cigarette on their lips, were pushing a heavy trolley overloaded with luggage. The passengers who had just landed in Tehran were practically running after them. Where we stood was about ten centimetres higher than the street level.

The two drivers had to take the luggage-laden trolley to the street level to load into their taxis. Suddenly, one of the wheels at the front of the trolley slipped onto the road and the luggage started to collapse. The two of them managed to hold on to the load with a series of acrobatic moves. I said to the children: "They were in such a rush, they missed the pavement."

One of the drivers with the cigarette between his lips said for everyone to hear: "The curves of true love never did run smooth. I was looking at you. Mr Reza, I missed the pavement and overturned. I love you by Mola Ali."

Night – Outdoors – Backstage – House of Cinema Grand Fete

We were backstage with Cyrus Alvand at the House of Cinema Grand Fete, waiting for the presenter, Hossein Pakdel, to call us onstage to present the Best Director Award to Bahman Farmanara.

It was crowded and cluttered backstage. There were lots of people there for no apparent reason. Who had let them in anyway? They were there for autographs and photos. Backstage of all places, where one should feel calm. I was telling everyone that I would give autographs after the programme. Nearly everyone accepted, except for this one person who stuck like glue and would not let go, giving me advice in that hullabaloo.

He said: "When you get to high places, you mustn't let it go to your head and act arrogant. You must answer to us."

Day – Outdoors – Vahdat Hall Courtyard

It was Khosrow Shakibai's funeral service. Everyone had attended and a large crowd was there. The courtyard of the Vahdat Hall and all the surrounding streets were packed with people who loved Khosrow and the cinema. Chairs had been placed in front of the stairs outside and the area had been closed off with guardrails. Many were sitting on the chairs, but the place was overcrowded with no more standing room. The pressure from those on their feet was so much that the guardrails finally broke.

I noticed Mehrdad MirKiani and Shalizeh Arefpour. They said it is not possible to move forward. Parviz Parastui was moderating the ceremony. He had shouted so much, he was losing his voice. I was standing in a corner of the courtyard with Yasamin Maleknasr, Gohar Kheirandish, and Mahmoud Pakniat. The crowd around us kept growing every minute, and amid all this there were those who wanted photos and autographs.

It was impossible to move. Every now and then, a few hands would come from behind with a mobile and take a photo. An elderly lady was standing next to me. I do not know why she had come and where she found the stamina. She was being crushed. There was pressure from all sides. She protested at the person behind me who had forced his arm forward over my shoulder with his mobile phone to take a picture and yelled at him to stop pushing.

The man holding the mobile said: "It's up to God!"

Parviz was shouting in the loudspeakers and inviting people to calm down and be orderly. He shouted like the refrain of a song: Be an Iranian. I hear a compatriot from Azarbaijan saying: "Where else are we from?"

I forced my way through the crowd and into the street from where I was standing and went home. I did not go to Behesht Zahra Cemetery. Hafez Ahmadi had called from there to say that the place was packed.

A few hours later, Ahad Sadeghi rang from Behesht Zahra to ask where I was. He said: "Come to the grave. Parviz has announced your name to come and talk. People are making way."

Very Early Morning – the Street

At nights, we were filming the "Mokhtarnameh" series by Davood Mir-Bagheri on location in Ahmadabad-e Mostowfi. We finished shooting around three or four in the morning and were on our way home.

The driver who was taking me home was a young man.

The journey was a long one and drivers are in a rush to take their passengers to their destination at that time of morning and go home. As a result, he was also careless at times.

When we arrived in the city, the young driver went through a red traffic light. I was about to protest, when he said: "Did you know that most accidents happen at this time of morning?"

I said: "So, why do you go through red traffic lights?"

He said: "Oh Sir, is everything else going right except for this!"

Night – Outdoors – Shandiz

Sarah and Ilia had gone to Mashhad. They decided to go to Shandiz restaurant with Zohreh and Mahbanou, my brother's wife and daughter. They sit in one of the restaurant's courtyards and wait for their dinner to be served.

Mahbanou, who is seven, was playing around the tables. A few ladies, upon seeing her, say: "O what a pretty girl. What's your name?"

Mahbanou: "Mahbanou."

The ladies: "Your name is as pretty as yourself. What's your surname?"

Mahbanou: "Kianian."

The ladies: "Goodness! You're probably going to say that you're related to Reza Kianian next!"

Mahbanou carries on playing without saying anything.

Sarah calls her and says: "Mahbanou sweetheart! You could have said that Reza is your uncle."

Mahbanou: "Nobody believes me. Nobody believes me at school or in our area. Only our neighbours believe me, because they've seen uncle Reza at our house."

The daughter of Reza Navab-Tehrani has the same problem. One night, she said: "Uncle, nobody believes that I know you."

I said: "But sweetheart, we have a photograph together."

She said: "They say it's been photoshopped."

She is only eight.

Another night, our neighbour's son came and said: "Mr Reza, can we go some place together, like a coffee shop, where the guys from our university can come and meet you?"

I said: "Ask your university to invite me so that I can come there."

He said: "No, I just want to show you to a few friends of mine. They won't believe that we're your neighbours."

Day – Indoors – Rasht

Jahanguir restaurant is famous in Rasht, and an old one. We went there with Hayedeh and Ali many moons ago.

Jahanguir himself would sit by the door, look at the customers from head to toe, and say: "Go downstairs, go upstairs, or go to the middle floor." He took a look at me, Hayedeh, and Ali, and said: "Go there." He showed us the middle floor. It was a mezzanine. We climbed the stairs. It was a full house. There was room, but we had to share a table with some other customers.

We turned around and said: "There are no free tables."

He said: "It is what it is."

We left hungry and upset.

A few years later, when I had become famous, we went to Jahanguir's again with Ali, Hayedeh, her mother, and Mehdi's family, her brother. It was a Friday. It was really busy when we arrived. We joined the end of a line of customers who were waiting for a table.

Some people would recognise me and start chatting. The customers would kindly tell us to move up the queue. And I would thank them, until Jahanguir arrived. He said a loud hello, and added: "Why are you standing in the queue? Come on up."

I said: "Thank you very much. There's more than a few of us, and we'll wait for our turn like everybody else. It's not nice to jump the queue."

Jahanguir addressed the people standing in line and yelled: "Does anyone mind that I take Mr Reza and his family in without waiting in the queue?"

Everyone said: "No, please go in."

Jahanguir said: "There you go. Any objections?"

We thanked everyone and went upstairs. We sat at the table and waited for the kebab and rice. Hayedeh and I remembered the first time we had been there.

Ali and I were sitting at a separate table. The food arrived and we started eating when Jahanguir came to our table carrying a deep, wide-rimmed dish and placed it in front of us. It was a dish of kebabs.

I said: "We've been served." And I showed him the food.

He said: "Eat up. Eat these. They're special," and he left.

I ate a piece of the chenjeh kebab that Jahanguir had brought. It was first class. Scrumptious. It was different from all the chenjeh kebabs I had ever eaten.

I told Ali: "Take some of this." He did and I took the rest to the table where Hayedeh and everyone else were sitting and passed it around.

Three years ago, we went to Jahanguir's with Mostafa Dashti, Taha Shojanouri, and Nariman Hamed. He had demolished the old restaurant and built a new one. We went in. He was not there. His son was sitting at the desk. He recognised and welcomed me.

The kebab he brought for us was very good, but not like the one Jahanguir had served me and Ali.

Everyone else enjoyed it very much, but my standards had changed. When I was full and had paid the bill, I asked his son: "Where is Mr Jahanguir?"

He said: "In the kitchen."

I went to the kitchen to see Jahanguir. After an almighty hello, he said: "Please go inside. I'll bring the food out in a minute."

"You were missed at the table. We've already eaten. We're going now." I said.

He was very upset and said: "Next time you're here, you'll come into the kitchen first and then you'll go into the restaurant."

"Sure, absolutely."

We said goodbye and left.

The following year, we went to his place again with Mostafa. I went into the kitchen first. I saw Jahanguir and we said "How's it going?" and then we went in and sat at our table. Jahanguir himself served the food. It was the same dish that I could not get out of mind.

Mostafa, who is a good cook and makes delicious kebabs, said: "I've never eaten a kebab like this one. It's a taste of heaven."

Day – Outdoors – Indoors – Enghelab Street

In Enghelab Street, I got into an Imam Hossein-Enghelab shuttle taxi and sat in the front seat.

Three ladies were sitting in the back. From their looks into the rear-view mirror and the whispering, I could tell that they had recognised me and were talking about me.

The driver was quiet and looking straight ahead. He was sour-faced and bad-tempered.

After a few minutes, the ladies started talking to me with an icebreaker. They asked about my movies and serials, and expressed their interest. I would thank them and they would talk. But the driver only looked straight ahead, as if he was in another world. Most drivers join in the conversations inside their taxi. But he seemed to have closed his ears to everything. I do not know what was going on in his mind. Whatever it was, he was miles away.

Sitting in the front, I'd occasionally turn around and answer the questions the ladies asked.

It said on the windshield: "Fare 250 tomans/person". I thought to myself: "How much 50 toman change does the driver need to have to give to his passengers!" I did not have 50 tomans.

The ladies were silent. I did not dare look into the mirror, because I had noticed that one of them was staring at me with a permanent smile. She was waiting to catch my eye and start again. We were finally outside Tehran University. I asked the driver to drop me off. He stopped. I gave a 500 toman note and got off. I was waiting for my change. He looked around in his change, but could not put together 50 tomans. Without looking at me, he gave me 300 in change. I gave him back 100 and said to keep the change.

The driver was not expecting this. He looked at me and was going to say something when he recognised me!

He said: "Oh, wow ... It's you! I'm sorry, I didn't recognise you at first, and he returned the money."

"No, please. Thank you." I said.

I did not take the money. As I was leaving, he said in a hurry: "Well now, there's a memory being made today with you getting in my car!"

Night – Indoors – Mehrabad Airport

A few years back, we were waiting at Mehrabad Airport with Hayedeh and Ali to pick up Sanam from Paris.

She was studying at the Conservatoire de Paris. She played the cello and was coming to Iran for her holidays.

People chatted to me until the plane landed and the passengers disembarked.

Those meeting the passengers made a corridor for them to pass with their trolleys and luggage.

Sanam arrived. We kissed and said hello. I took her suitcase and we left.

Sanam was carrying her cello on her shoulder like a backpack.

As we walked, I could hear the voices of a couple of other people. One of them said: "It's his daughter, right?"

The other one said: "Yes, I know her."

The first one said: "Why has she got such a large guitar?"

The other one said: "Well, she's Kianian's daughter after all."

Day – Outdoors – Bahar Street

Bahar is a northbound one-way street. It is full of corner shops, green grocers, and boiler accessory shops. This is why there are always a number of coke, milk, or mineral water delivery trucks double-parked on the street, vans unloading fruits outside the green grocers, or uploading boiler accessories. Shoppers are also double-parked to do their shopping.

Driving on Bahar Street is like an assault course. There are also pedestrians crossing the street, including old men women, and children. To go from bad to worse, there are always a number of motorbikes driving in the opposite direction as an integral part of Bahar Street, because there is a courier service there. Moving on Bahar Street is like being in a dynamic computer game. The only difference is that the game takes place in a virtual world and annihilating double-parked cars, motorbikes going down the wrong way, and pedestrians who do not use the zebra crossing, earns you points. But Bahar Street is not a virtual world. The points you earn are the other way around!

As I was there one day as usual, I was steering my car clear of a double-parked dairy van with great acrobatics when a speeding oncoming motorbike tried to pass between my car and the van. There was no room. He signalled at me to give way. It was an impossible task. I said: "You're driving in the wrong direction; move to one side and let me pass."

I continued to drive. The biker was forced to back up and I drove past. I could hear him swear. Like always, I turned a deaf ear. When I reached the end of Bahar Street and was going to turn into Bahar-e Shiraz, there was a bottleneck - same old same old. I was waiting for the traffic to debottleneck when I heard the side-view mirror of my car shatter. I saw that the same biker had followed me and shattered my mirror for revenge. I got out immediately. He was in such haste that he was unable to run away and fell in a turn he was trying to make. He left his bike and started to run. He stopped a little further. The bottleneck at the end of Bahar Street was loosening up. A few cars drove away and the others stuck behind me started to honk. They recognised me as soon as they saw me and came to see what had happened. They would say hello in the commotion and some would even embrace me. The biker walked towards me and said: "I'm sorry. I've just recognised you. None of this mess would have happened if you had introduced yourself in the first place!"

Day – Outdoors – A Street in Tehran

It is a one-way street near 7th Tir Square. It is my regular gateway home. There is always an oncoming car or motorbike. Most of the time, I give way for them to pass, because I believe evil must be avoided. Or to put it better, one must slip by and pass. At times when I am angry, I will not give way and wait for them to back up and let me pass. Of course, a few insults always see me off!

Just a few days ago, as I was driving through the same place, a few motorbikes speedily turned into the one-way street. Although I am always careful, I was taken by surprised and honked my horn continuously at them. They drove past without paying any attention to me or the sound of the horn. One of them stopped. I asked him: "Do you know that this is a one-way street?"

He said: "Of course I do."

He was an old man whose grey hair showed from underneath the helmet. I had nothing more to say. But he continued: "Mr Reza, how are you? Do you still live in the same place?"

And then added: "Don't you remember me? I sent you tonnes of Godly love."

A car honked behind me to open the way. I started to move. The old man yelled: "You make such a face. I'm talking to you…"

I moved on. I looked at him in the rear-view mirror. He had moved on too.

Day – Outdoors – A Street in Tehran

The driver who took me to location every morning seemed like a polite man. He said he had spent a few years in Japan, saved some money, and returned to Iran. He was at the service of the film industry with his car.

He used to talk or ask questions about everything and everyone on the way to work. He also criticised our people very much for not respecting each other. We were stuck in a traffic jam close to location. He paused momentarily, looked around, pulled to the left - that is to the side of oncoming traffic – and tried to bypass the jam. His action only created another traffic jam on the other side. He tried to bypass that too, but it was already too late. Traffic came to a standstill on both sides of the street. I only looked at him. He said: "See, there's not an ounce of sacrifice left."

He was upset with everyone.

I said: "Our side was blocked, but the other side was moving. You went down the wrong way and caused a jam."

"I have work to do. I'm not an idler like them!"

Day – Outdoors – A Street in Tehran

I was waiting at the red traffic light. It was too hot. A minibus was standing next to me with the exhaust fumes wafting in directly through my window. I did not know which way to turn. I pulled up the window. But it became so hot in the car that I could feel sweat dripping down my neck from behind my ears straight away. My back clinging to the seat was soaking wet. I leaned forward towards the wheel to air my wet shirt and cool off. I remembered that I had pulled up the window. I looked at the light; it was still red. It had no countdown timer, so I did not know when it would turn green. The minibus exhaust was smoking. The driver pressed the gas pedal from time to time. I do not know why. He just emitted more fumes into the air. With the sound of a few horns coming from the cars behind, I realised that the light was green now. I put the car in first gear and waited for the cars in front to start moving. It was my turn at last. Just as soon as I reached the junction, a motorbike who had gone through the red light passed in front of me. I almost had an accident. I honked and the biker disappeared between the cars. I looked. A young traffic police was standing in the shade, engaged in conversation with someone. The only thing he was unaware of was the traffic and comings and goings of cars and motorcycles. I pulled over after the junction and stopped. I got out of the car and went to the traffic police. The person who was talking to him was delighted to see me and said hello. The traffic police also turned around. He recognised me as well, came towards me and said hello. I answered and asked: "Why are you standing here?"

He asked: "What do you mean?"

I pointed at the junction. Two other motorbikes were going through the red light at that very moment.

"Why won't you say anything to them. I almost had an accident just now."

The person talking to the traffic police said: "Don't sweat blood. Go act in your movies and delight us."

The traffic police also said: "Don't worry about them. How are you?"

"What are you here for? Why have they posted you here?" I said.

He said: "Nothing, scarecrow! They don't issue me with traffic tickets to give out. At least crows are afraid of scarecrows. This lot take no notice of us!"

Day – Outdoors – A Side Street off Bahar Street

There is a one-way side street off Bahar Street which leads to Shariati Street. As per routine, there is an adequate and reliable number of cars and motorcycles driving in the wrong direction. There are two types of offenders. The fair ones pull to one side when they see an oncoming car and give right of way, and then they carry on with their offence. But the "cool" – as they themselves claim - unfair offenders flash their lights and send Godly love your way with a smile, meaning "What can we do? There's no other way. This is no country…", and signal for you to pull to one side and let them pass!

One time, when I was driving in this side street in the right direction, one of the cool, unfair offenders flashed his lights. I continued to drive. And he came and flashed his lights, until we were toe-to-toe. Several cars were parked in the side street and there was room for only one to pass. With a brazen, "cool-filled smile!" he flashed his lights again, meaning just back up to a point where I can pass! I just stood there. The sun was shining on his windshield and I was in the light and shade. He flashed his lights a few more times. In the end, he got out of the car and walked towards me angrily to grab me by the collar. When he got to the car window, he recognised me. He collected himself a little, a smile demonstrating his coolness appeared on his lips again, and he said: "You too? You're a cultured person. You're a role model for society. We are the uncultured ones. Now back up so I can pass." Then he got into his car, put it in first gear and signalled at me to back up!

Day – Outdoors – Noon of Ashura –Street

It is beyond me why, but most people do not observe the law on official holidays, especially on eid days and religious holidays. They behave like Sunday drivers and go in any direction they please. One Ashura day, I was going home after having received some votive food at Hafez Ahmadi's house. The light turned red as I arrived at a junction. I braked and stopped. It seemed that the car behind me was not expecting me to stop, so it braked really hard to avoid hitting me.

It honked its horn for me to move on. I pointed at the red traffic light. He got out of the car and said as he was approaching: "I'm your humble servant; today belongs to Imam Hossein. There's no red and green lights. Keep moving."

As he got closer to me, he recognised me. He said hello, and added: "I was expecting more than this from you. A cool actor never stops at a red traffic light on Ashura day. Where is your Hosseini passion?"

Day – Outdoors – Indoors – Indoors – Tehran

We were working in the lobby of Laleh Hotel one day, when shooting for the movie "An Umbrella for Two." It was just a few simple shots and we were supposed to wrap up by noon. So, I was going to meet someone at four o'clock. But the work dragged on and would not finish on time.

I was in a rush and the production team called a taxi for me to make me feel at ease. The taxi was waiting outside the hotel for me to finish work and take me to my destination. Finally, we finished at three thirty in the afternoon. I cleaned my make up in a hurry, dressed up and ran to the taxi. One of the guys in logistics was kind enough to open the taxi door for me. I said goodbye and told the taxi to get going while I gave him the address as he pulled away.

He was driving and peeking at me every now and then. I thought he had recognised me and wants to talk. Close to Valiasr Sq, he finally asked: "Who are you?"

I said: "Why?"

"They kept me waiting outside the hotel for two hours for you. And then someone ran and opened the door for you." He said.

"We were working there."

"Doing what?"

At this point, I realised that he had not recognised me and is curious to know who I am.

"Shooting for a movie."

"You're a director."

"No."

"What then?"

"Actor."

"Aha." He looked at me closely, but did not recognise me. "Who else is in it?"

"Hedieh Tehrani." I thought he would surely know her.

"Which one?"

It was strange. He did not know her either.

"The actress."

He said: "There's only one actor for me in the world - Fardin. And that's that; and only one actor after the revolution - Amin Zendegani. And that's that."

Then, he said no more and just looked ahead.

After a while, he said without looking at me: "I saw a film with the late Fardin in it which turned my life around," and he made an "around" gesture at me with his hand.

"Which one?" I asked.

"I can't remember the title."

"Tell me the story. I'll give you the title."

He thought for a while, before saying: "I don't remember the story either!"

And he fell silent again, staring straight ahead. I wanted him to talk, so I said: "Did you go to the movies often?"

"I have many memories from the movies." He replied.

"Tell me about it."

"I was a kid. We lived in Tehran-Pars district. The place was deserted at the time. I went to school by bike. They were shooting in the wilderness of Tehran-Pars. I used to stop and watch on my way to school. Sometimes, I'd forget about school and watch the shooting."

He went silent and stared.

"And then?"

"One day, they were shooting a nudish scene. I stood and watched. Shahin was starring in it. Do you remember Shahin?"

"Yes. Which movie was it?"

"Shahin in a miniskirt (he placed his hand a little higher up his knee), up to here. She was almost naked."

And he went silent again and stared.

"What else?" I asked.

"The movies were in black and white in those days. Colour movies were new … Do you know how they made them in colour?"

"No, tell me."

"They had these devices. Like this … (he showed surfaces with his hands that looked like reflectors) … With this technique they redirected the coloured light on Shahin and shot a colour movie."

Regrettably, we had reached the destination. I would have liked to listen to him talk some more.

"I'll get off here."

He stopped. I said goodbye and got out. He just waved at me without looking and drove off.

Day – Indoors – My House

The master carpenter and his assistant were installing the closets I had ordered for my office. I have known the master carpenter for years. He does most of the work for the cinema crowd, but I was meeting his assistant for the first time. I could see that he was excited to see me and my house. A couple of hours went by and the ice melted. He started talking to me. He spoke with a lisp in a loutish accent.

He had seen the dotar I played in the film "The Red Ribbon". He pointed it out and said: "It plays then!?"

"Yes, it has frets on it. An Afghan man made if for me." I said.

The master carpenter said with a smile: "It's from 'The Red Ribbon' then?"

"Yes. It's a keepsake."

His assistant said: "If we decide to keep all the souvenirs, it'll take up a lot of space."

"I don't keep everything."

He said: "I have a mate who makes these too; dulcimers, violins, pianos … and the like!"

Day- Outdoors – 16th Azar Street

I wanted to park my car on 16th Azar Street on a Friday afternoon. I found a space on the right-hand side near Molavi Hall. I noticed the "No Parking" sign behind the branches and leaves of the tree and drove to the left hand side of the street where there was no sign. A series of red traffic cones lined the street. I parked between two of them. As I got out of the car, a traffic warden rushed towards me.

I said: "It's no parking on the other side. But there are no signs on this side."

He recognised me and said: "Well, well, what brings you to this part of the world?"

"I'm going to the theatre."

"Where!?"

I showed him Molavi Hall, and said: "There."

"Hold on." He then picked up the red cone from behind my car and placed it in the front, saying: "It's better now. It's no longer prohibited."

I thanked him and was about to leave when he said: "Where to?"

"The theatre."

He said: "Give us your mobile number if there's anything we need."

"Like what?"

"For a ceremony."

"What kind of ceremony?" I asked.

"A wedding!"

"Your son or daughter?"

"No man. The weddings of friends and family; you can come and play theatre!"

"Thanks for your concern."

"We look after our artists!" He said.

Day – Outdoors – Tehran

My classmate from my university days, Rana Bastani, had come to Iran from the US after many long years. She was now a vegetarian. We went to the Yogi coffee shop at the Iranian Artists' House and she had a vegetarian kebab and rice! I was not sure why a vegetarian would fancy kebab and rice.

On our way back, we had to drive through the streets of Mirdamad to drop her off. I was driving slowly and carefully so as not to scare her. Those who have been away from Iran for long years are bound to be terrified of its streets.

I turned towards Mina Roundabout from Haghani Motorway. This small roundabout is a strange one. Traffic comes in from three sides and leaves from only one exit. It did not even have a sign at the time indicating that this is a roundabout. As a result you could turn left and exit from it. Please believe me, I always went around it. I am always a law-abiding citizen. But I am not sure what happened on that night which caused a traffic jam and I turned left. I will say this one more time: It had no roundabout sign in those days. As soon as I took the only exit out, I saw a police car and motorcycle there, fining those who had come in from the left. I was ready to say there is no roundabout sign, and then get a ticket. One of the policemen came up to me. Americans are petrified of the police. Rana was scared too. The policeman recognised me and gave me a military salute! I answered back and apologised, explaining that there was no sign and that I always went round the...

But I saw that the policeman went and brought his superior officer. He also gave me a military salute and said: "You may go this time." It meant that I would not be fined! I thanked him and was about to leave, when he asked: "Where are you going?" I said: "A couple of streets further down." He said: "I'll send an escort if you have a long way to go." I was dying of shame. I said: "No, thank you. It's not far." He kept insisting and I kept saying no. Until he agreed that I should go without an escort.

Rana who had been scared at first and then surprised, was now confused. She kept looking at me in astonishment.

Day – Outdoors - Amādgāh Street in Isfahan

Hayedeh, Ali and I were coming out of Abbasi Hotel and crossing the street. A young girl was filming with her camcorder. She noticed me and turned it towards me until we had reached the pavement on the other side and walked past her. As we walked away, she ran towards us and called me. She apologised profusely to me and Hayedeh for taking up our time and continued in an attractive Shirazi accent by saying she had a small request. I thought she wanted an autograph. I said: "Please give me your notebook to sign." She said: "I don't want an autograph. Please, just act a little bit for me right here so I can film you!"

Day – Indoors – Kashan Bazaar

We were walking in the bazaar with Hayedeh, Ali, Mostafa,

Sa'ad, Golnar, and Gandom. Many people were greeting us and saying hello. Among them a young shopkeeper, who told me: "Have you seen the stone mill in this place?" I had not seen it and it sounded interesting to me. We all wanted to see the stone mill. We followed the young man. As we entered the mill, it was as if we had stepped back a century in time. It was a dark environment lit with two columns of natural light from the ceiling with dust floating in them. There was a circular platform over which another large circular stone revolved and milled everything in-between. There were many bags piled up around the place, plus a short man there who was the miller. There were only two signs in the place indicating that it existed in this century: one was the engine which turned the stone instead of a horse or a mule, and the other a 60W lamp which was on, but did not emit much light.

The young man tapped the short man on the shoulder and pointed at us. He turned around, looked at us, and saw me. He walked towards me, shook hands, and embraced me on the spot. He drew the frame of a television screen with his index fingers in the air, pursed his lips, took a kiss form his lips with the fingers of his right hand and blew it at me, meaning that he likes me. Then he started giving explanations about his place of work with other hand gestures. He talked so much and I talked to him so much with gestures that the rest of the company got tired. He went quiet and said goodbye to us with another kiss and we left.

To this day, Mostafa draws a frame in the air with his hands every time he sees me and blows a kiss.

Day – Outdoors – 7th Tir Square in Tehran

The traffic congestion charge had just been implemented and I did not have a permit to enter the area although I lived in it, and still do. The police had stopped me on a number of occasions, but had let me go without a fine when they recognised me. One day when I felt reassured that no one would fine me, I drove into 7th Tir Square. I circled the square and exited down Mofateh Street.

The police saw me and signalled for me to stop. I stopped and said hello to the officer with a smile. The expression on his face did not change. He asked for my licence and documents as I stared into his eyes so that perhaps he might recognise me. I gave him my driving licence hoping that he would recognise my name and forget the ticket. Without reacting, he filled in the ticket and handed it to me with my licence. Hopeless, I started to leave when he asked: "By the way Mr Kianian, what's the name of your new movie?"

Night – Outdoors – Sohrehvardi Street – Tehran

I was driving home at two thirty in the morning in that same black and silver Nissan Patrol. The streets were empty and barely a car passed by. The light turned red at the junction as I drove up. I stopped. In the dead of night, a Hillman Paykan also pulled up and stopped next to me. I could only see the car roof. The light turned green and we started to move. At the next junction, the light turned red again. I stopped. A lorry speeded right through the red light. Then, the Paykan drove up slowly and stopped. Just then, the sound of loudspeakers broke the silence of the night and my sobriety. The voice said: "Your obedient servant, Mr Reza!" I jumped up and looked around. It was the sound of the police loudspeaker coming from that same Paykan standing next to me. The light turned green and the police Paykan drove off. At the next junction, the light was green, but the police had stopped the lorry, and I drove past with a wave and a smile.

Day – Outdoors – Bahar Street – Tehran

I was on foot. I wanted to go to the other side of the street and get some cash from the bank. The street was busy and not so easy to cross. I kept walking up and down until I succeeded to reach the other side. As luck would have it, I had used the zebra crossing. I went into the bank. I said hello to the employees and joined the queue. Suddenly, a jolly elderly man said out loud: "Well done to this actor! Because he kept going up and down the street until he was able to use the zebra crossing and then joined the queue at the bank like everyone else. Then he walked up to me, shook hands and introduced himself. He was a retired police sergeant.

From that day on, I have always tried to use the zebra crossing.

Day – Outdoors – Around Asalem – Northern Iran

We were planning to go to Asalem beach with Nariman, Teh, and Mostafa; to the same place where tree stumps have emerged from the water and are covered in green moss. Mostafa was driving. He stopped on the side of the road and asked a local man who was passing by: "Which one is the old Asalem road?" With a northern accent, he answered: "The Asalem-Khalkhal road is on that side." I said: "I'd like to go to the beach." He showed me the new paved road. I asked where is the old road? He paused, stared at me, and yelled: "Bravo! The special actor!"

Teh said: "We had mushrooms and onions too!"

Day – Indoors – Noshahr

I was with Mostafa. It was two in the afternoon and we were both starving. We had the address of a restaurant and were hurrying towards it. A young passer-by saw me, came up to me, greeted me and asked for permission to take a picture with me. He prepared his mobile, gave it to Mostafa, stood by my side and placed his arm around my shoulder, saying take it. At this moment, a shopkeeper who was standing outside his shop ran towards us, stood next to us and said: "With your permission, I'll share in your happiness!" He did not know the young man and the photo was taken with his mobile. I am convinced that photo will never reach him. He just wanted to be registered somewhere, because he did not know me either!

Day – Outdoors – Taleghani Street – Tehran

"The Apartment" series was being aired and I had just become famous.

I was driving on Taleghani Street with my Renault 5. A grey Peugeot was driving alongside me; one those given to officials in the government sector. The seating arrangement of the passengers was very interesting. A "framed" government official wearing a granddad collar and a suit jacket with a trimmed beard was at the wheel. A fifteen or sixteen-year-old boy with a soft, patchy stubble sat next to him, wearing a suit and a white shirt. Two women sat in the back wearing the black chador, the head cover under the chador, glasses, and black gloves. It was obvious that one was the mother of the family and the other the marriageable young daughter. Everything was self-explanatory and complete, as if a set and costume designer had arranged the whole thing.

The woman gestured at her husband. The husband looked at me and signalled to pull over. It made me nervous. I thought perhaps I had upset them by looking at them. What was I to do? I had landed myself in hot water. I pressed down on the accelerator and drove off, ignoring them. The Peugeot pulled in front of me on the other side of the junction and forced me to stop. So many different thoughts flashed through my mind at that moment. I concocted a lot of stories to tell them; that I had no bad intentions when I looked at them. I got out of the car, ready to explain myself. They go out too; first the woman, then the daughter, and finally the husband and son. Before I could open my mouth, they started greeting me, praising the series I was in and my role as Manouchehr. Then, the official complained that I had ignored them and why did I snub people? I swallowed all the explanations I had prepared. The woman and the girl were standing so close to me, as if I was their close male relative. The husband and the son did not even mind or give a warning ... They left after I gave them an autograph and I was left with a pile of questions.

When I got home, I recounted the whole story for Hayedeh and how their friendly behaviour had shocked me. As always, Hayedeh had a logical explanation. She said: "They don't wear the hijab when they watch you at home. They watch you without their hijabs and identify with you. So they think of you as a mahram.

Day – Night – Indoors – Outdoors – Tehran

After the very popular series "The Final Shot", in which I played an addict, many people thought that I was actually an addict!

1. I was walking on Mofateh Street one day when a strapping, chubby man grabbed my wrist. He was wearing a gold watch and a big gold necklace, with an open collar and a big belly. He insisted on taking me into a large car showroom, and told everyone: "I've got him!" I was scared. He told me: "Well done. I've told this lot many times that you don't know the pain of withdrawal symptoms. When your series was aired, I could show them how painful it is. Well done. I'm your humble servant!" He forced me to sit down and offered me tea. I remembered the movie "Morphine" that I had seen as a young lad, in which the late Mohammad-Ali Jafari featured and scared me of addiction for life.

2. I wanted to buy a T-shirt on Churchill Street, when a street peddler came up to me, said hello and pulled me to one side: "I never want to see you suffer the shakes. I'm your humble servant anytime you need more make up. You just come to me; I'm your man!"

3. A luxury Mercedes Benz braked in front of me on Takht-e Tavous Street. Three jolly people were its passengers; those who have dyed, pitch black hair like the feathers of a black crow. They opened the door and invited me to accompany them. They said they were going to have fun and games, and had all sorts of wraps!

4. On our way to the seaside in the north, I had parked the car for a rest when we arrived on Imamzadeh Hashem hill. I was with my family. An old man from the village walked up to me, took me by the collar, and said: "If you hadn't punched the leader of Siavash Tahmures's gang, I'd slap you so hard that you'd remember it for the rest of your days." Then he hugged and kissed me, and advised me to give up drugs!

5. In the series, I also forged birth certificates and passports. I was stopped on a number of occasions by people who wanted forged passports, offering me all the money I wanted!

6. A friend of the family, Sholeh Nabavi, came to our place once and said she had gone to the hairdresser's to cut her hair. The hairdresser has asked her: "Do you want it 'Jamshidi' style?" When she had asked what Jamishidi was, the hairdresser has said like Jamshid the forger in the series "The Final Shot".

I realised later that the "Jamshidi" hairstyle had become popular for both men and women.

Night – Indoors – Outdoors – Imam Reza Shrine

1. We were sitting in front of the latticed mausoleum in Imam Reza's shrine with my friend Khosro Nikamouz, immersed in ourselves, when a hand came between us from behind with a pen and paper, and a voice said: "Stick an autograph on here will you!" I am not sure since when you have to "stick" autographs. At this time, a few more people surrounded us for autographs. Khosro, who had lost his peace, said: "You ought to be ashamed of yourselves. You have to get Imam Reza's autograph in here, and Reza Kianian's outside." When we left the mausoleum, the same people came and got their autographs. From that day forward, I never gave autographs inside Imam Reza's shrine.

2. Another time, when I had gone to the shrine alone, I was giv-

ing autographs outside and the crowd just got bigger. Many who did not know what was happening also stood around and asked for autographs just in case; it was the same mindset that had developed after coupons had to be used when food was rationed: We just stood in queues without knowing what was happening in the hope that we might get a morsel of something. An elderly lady from the village also managed to move forward in the crowd and say: "Write a prayer for me too." She thought I was giving prayers out to people. One of the "devotee servants of the shrine" came to disperse the crowd, and asked: "What's going on here." He thought people wanted prayers from me. Somebody said: "He's writing prayers." He dispersed the crowd and came towards me to arrest me, but I ran away into the crowd.

Night – Indoors – Outdoors – Mashhad

I watched the Iran-US football match at the 1998 FIFA World Cup at the house of my belated parents, may they rest in peace. When Iran scored the first goal, I screamed with joy and covered my mouth straight away so as not to wake up my parents who were asleep. I was sure my mother was awake, because the slightest noise always woke her up. After the match and Iran's win, I called Khosro to go out. We watched the people celebrate on the streets. The first place we went to was the shrine, which was packed. A bunch of people were doing the Mexican wave in front of the latticed mausoleum, and shouting: "Reza, Reza, we thank you!" And then we went to the streets uptown. A group of young people recognised me at the end of Sajjad Boulevard. They started switching lanes and tailgating us. The number of those who identified us increased, creating a traffic jam, and the street came to a standstill. Not one car could move now. Many young people got out of their cars, shouting: "Reza must dance!"

Day- Night – Outdoors –Streets of Tehran

After the series "Young Lawyers" - in which I had a law firm and tried to serve the people with a group of young colleagues – I found many clients on the streets who wanted me to take up their case. Once, on Jam Street, a well-dressed man with a Samsonite got out of his car in a hurry and stopped me. He introduced himself. He had a trading company and said his partners had ripped him off of his shares and driven him bankrupt by falsifying records. He placed his brief case on the bonnet of the car and opened it. It was filled with a myriad documents. He pleaded with me to accept his case. He said he had seen on TV that my colleagues and I had clean hands; that we were honourable lawyers who did not take bribes. He said he had been trying to find me for a long time. When I listened to him talk, I realised why he had been cheated by his partners and lost everything.

Day – Outdoors – A Hill in Kurdistan

We were on location for the film "A Little Kiss", shooting the graveyard scene. The weather was cold beyond words! A few space heaters had been brought for Ms Khorvash and placed around her so that she could say her lines. It was winter and the days were short. As we had little natural light, it was decided to have lunch at four in the afternoon and make the most of what light we had.

I was already famished at two in the afternoon. I asked the people in logistics to give me some bread and yoghurt to calm the burning sensation in my stomach. I stood behind one of the cars to eat my yoghurt. Payam Dehkordi also joined me and we shared it. One of the local villagers who was helping us out thought we were secretly eating bread and yoghurt. He came to us and asked: "Don't they feed you?" He felt really sorry for us. An hour later, he asked me: "Are you happy in your job?" I said: "Yes." He said: "It's a tough job." I said: "But your job is tougher." He said: "No my man. We work for a few months and spend the rest of the time with our wife and kids."

The scenes for Ms Khorvash were shot and she was sent to take a rest. It was my turn. The sun was setting and a shadow pulled over the mountain little by little. Mahmoud Kelari walked ahead of the shadow with his cameras and reflectors and kept telling me to move ahead. I'd say a sentence and the shadow would catch up with us. Then I'd move over and say the next sentence. Bahman Farmanara also directed me from behind the camera. I was shaking and trying to control myself while I talked with an imagined Ms Khorvash. The same local villager who was watching the scene lost his temper and shouted: "For goodness' sake, leave this poor man alone. You won't give him food. He's not even wearing any decent clothing and you keep telling him to move here and there, don't say it this way, say it that way. What's he, a slave?"

Day – Outdoors – Amir Atabak Street – Tehran

I was going home with the shopping. A young woman said hello at the top of Amir Atabak Street, and added domineeringly: "Please stop." I answered her hello and stopped.

She said: "I saw your movie." And fell silent, staring at me. I knew which movie she was talking about. It was a bad one and, fortunately, was not seen much. I said: "I'm sorry." This is my maxim and solves many problems. She said: "Yes, it wasn't a very good movie at all. It was bad." And she continued: "I saw it because you were in it and I was really upset when I left the movies." She went quiet, swallowed her anger, and said: "If you act in one more movie like this one … that'll be it!"

And she left.

Day – Night – Indoors – Outdoors – Many Places

One day many years ago, when I'd just become famous, I was sitting at the wheel of my green Renault 5 in the traffic of Beheshti Street. A young boy wanted to clean the windscreen of my car.

But he paused just as soon as he saw me, and asked: "Are you an actor?" I said yes. He asked: "What's your name?" I said: "You tell me." He said: "What does it start with?" I said: "K". He said: "Katibaei?"

I have been called by the names of other actors many times and asked for an autograph. At first, I'd explain to them that I am not Hashempour; I'm not Gharibian, Entezami, Nasiri, Rashidi … I am Reza Kianian. But as time passed, I no longer insisted, and still don't. I answer to all the names and give the autographs. I have given many autographs on behalf of many people, even Majid Entezami. But one day an elderly lady called me Tehrani and asked me for an autograph. So I signed my name for her as Hedieh Tehrani.

Day – Outdoors – Kashan

We had stepped out of the Amir Kabir Hotel in Kashan with Hayedeh and Ali and were walking towards Fin Garden. A man, whose wife was riding pillion with him, recognised me. He told his wife: "Look, it's him." His wife did not understand who he was talking about.

The husband pointed at me again with his head because his hands were tied, saying: "This one."

The woman missed it again

The husband finally stopped a little ahead of us and said to me: "Come here."

I could still the whole thing from the corner of my eye, but pretended not to and carried on as though nothing was happening.

The man on the motorbike yelled at me: "I'm telling you to come over here!"

I jumped over the narrow water canal and went towards them.

The biker said to his wife: "Do you see? It's him." The woman saw me and shook her head at the man to say: "You're right."

And the man speeded away.

Sunset – Indoors – Mirak Gallery – Mashhad

The "Anbouh"[4] group photography exhibition had been organised by the late Mohsen Rasoulof. Mohsen had such passion for life and was so young that no one believed he would leave us so soon. I had two works on show. It was my first photography exhibition.

As it happens, I was in Mashhad on opening day and welcoming visitors to the exhibition.

A group of young girls arrived and were excited and emotional to see me. The eldest one told me: "My father tells me that he's hit you in elementary school. Every time you're on TV he says I've hit this one."

All of a sudden, time rewound many years. She was right. I told her she was right and then asked her surname. I told them I'd never been in a scuffle with anyone in my life, except that one time that your father is talking about. I was extremely shy as a small boy. Every time we had guests or I had a problem, I'd go to the basement of our house. There were two chests there. One was almost empty. I'd go inside that one, close the lid, and cry. My mother who knew my hiding place would come just in time, console me, and take me out of there.

On that day, a ceremony was being held in our school and everyone had been given an Iranian flag; a paper flag which had been glued to a small straw. In Mashhad, we called those straws "Lukh".

I had been able to collect four flags. I was happy and when school was out I was walking home with the flags in my hand. I was kind of chubby before puberty; a shy little boy with cheeks

---
4 Mass

hanging down and a shaved head.

My mother always told me: "Never fight with anyone. If anyone swears at you, don't answer back. If anyone hits you, don't hit them back. God will punish them." The teachings of my mother, may her soul rest in peace, had such impact on me that I have never raised my hand to anyone to this day that I am in the fifth decade of my life. I was walking home on that day happy with my four flags. Two boys from the school stopped me and asked me to give them my flags. There was no reason why I should. I did not give them the flags; they jumped on me, beat me up, took the flags, and left.

I was disconsolate. I had been beaten and lost my flags too. I could have beaten them up. I could beat them both. But my mother's teachings had affected me to such an extent that I could not raise my hand to beat anyone. This is mostly why I was so sad. Although I could have beaten them and I was stronger, I had been beaten and lost my flags. My clothes were dusty too.

I got home and went straight to the basement. I took refuge in my chest of loneliness, closed the top and cried to my heart's content.

Until I heard my mother's kind voice. She would sit on the other chest and talk to me.

I told that girl: "Give my best to your father and tell him you were not alone that day. You were with one of your mates. It took the two of you to beat Reza."

Afternoon – Outdoors – Tehran

A veteran soldier of the imposed war came forward, we said hello and chatted. I say soldier because the way he looked and was dressed reminded one of the films about the sacred defence. His appearance had not changed in the slightest. We had a heart-to-heart, and then he said: "I have a message to deliver to you." I said: "What?"

I was intrigued.

He said: "May all your dearly departed rest in peace. When my mother watched "The Glass Agency", she recommended that I invite you to our home to sit at our spread. I did not find you. My grandmother passed away a few years ago. It's too late, but I still delivered the message to you. May she rest in peace, she was a great fan of yours."

Day – Outdoors – Indoors – Street – Taxi

I was waiting for a taxi. A lady on the pavement addressed me out loud: "May you never be without a car." I said hello and replied: "With this traffic, it's easier to travel by taxi."

I noticed a taxi stop and say: "Get in Mr Reza."

I wanted to name my destination; he said: "Get in."

I sat in the front. I said hello and gave him the address of my destination.

He started talking, moaning, criticising, and asking. He was a professional movie watcher. It was obvious from what he said that he was a movie-goer before and after the revolution.

He said: "Business is bad, and it's getting worse by the day. I have to kiss this job goodbye next year." I asked: "Why? There are more and more taxis every day. There are so many private taxi companies." He showed me a green taxi for women with a woman driver and said: "Because of them."

I said: "But they have nothing to do with you."

He said: "They're shy for now. But they'll be brazen by next year and then there'll be no stopping them. The women are taking over."

I said: "You can stay home and rest for a while. Let them do the work. It's not that bad!"

He said: "That's the way it's going, you can be sure of that. But a thousand tomans earned by a man goes a longer way than a hundred thousand tomans made by a woman."

I asked: "But why?"

He said: "Why state the obvious? The facts speak for themselves. You don't need a reason for it!"

He talked some more and said: "You'll be out of a job soon too. The women have taken over everything. Look at the movie titles: 'One Women, Two Women, Three Women'; 'There Is Always a Woman In-Between'; 'Women Are Angels'."

Afternoon – Outdoors – Mashhad

It was the month of Ramadan. We had all gone to Mashhad for the fortieth day of my mother's passing. We were all at her house; a house we knew we had to vacate after the ceremony.

We were all rushing around to make sure the fortieth ceremony would be organised and go well. Vahid and I went out to buy fruits and sweets. Marzieh rang and said: "Buy some sweet flat, Shirmal bread for iftar, just like the old days when father used to come to iftar with Shirmal bread."

When we were done shopping, we went and stood in the bread line after we parked the car. The people in the line said hello to me and offered that I should not stand in the queue and move to the front of the line. I stood where I was and thanked them, until the baker noticed me. He called me with a gesture. I went forward and said hello. He answered by nodding and signalled that I should stay there … Then he gestured to ask how many I wanted.

"Ten." I said.

He nodded to say that he had understood.

He talked to me with gestures, but used language with the other customers.

The bread was finally ready. He placed them in front of me. I took out my wallet and asked: "How much?"

He looked at me with reproach and signalled that I should leave.

I was confused. I asked again: "Sorry, how much should I offer?"

There was more reproach in his eyes this time. He added hand gestures to those of the head and eyes, meaning shame on you; go. You're my guest. I thanked him and turned around to leave. I heard the person who was working at the automated bread oven say: "Quite an actor. He's a child of Meshhad[5]."

Night – Outdoors – Tehran

In the murderous rush hour traffic of Shariati Street, just before Mirdamad where the street had been blocked to build the underground station, there was a deviation where I had to turn into a side street. All those cars had to turn into a narrow street. We moved centimetre by centimetre. The car in front moved forward a little and I followed suit. A voice said: "So would heaven and earth have met if you'd let me pass? Would the nuclear bomb be late in the making!"

My side window was open. I looked and saw two people on a motorcycle. The driver who had come out of that narrow one-way street, wanted to go up Shariati. It was an old man. I said: "You seem to be going down the wrong way."

The person in the back smiled when he saw me; more than usu-

---
5 "Meshhad" in Mashhadi pronunciation

al. He was also a grown man. He said: "Hello Mr Reza. How are you? I take my hat off to you. Apologies; Gholami did not recognise you."

And then he turned to the driver of the motorbike: "Pull yourself together man. You came down the wrong way."

Then he said to me: "Gholami is a cool guy. He's just confused."

Day – Outdoors – 1000-Bed Hospital

If somebody wants a picture with me on the street, especially in busy places, I will apologise and say: "If it starts, it will never end."

Once, when I was leaving the 1000-bed hospital with Davoud Amiri, a man and a woman ran towards me breathless and asked for a keepsake photo. As always, I apologised to them, pointing at the crowd and saying: "If it starts, it will never end!"

The woman whispered something to the man. The man looked around quickly, and said in my ear: "I fully understand. You take the last one with us!!!"

Day – Outdoors – Enghelab Club

I was returning from exercising. One of the guys working at the club said to me angrily: "Every time you're on TV, my little girl won't let us change the channel. She keeps watching until the TV blows up."

Day – Outdoors – Narenj Townlet

A little boy of five or six stopped me and said: "I know you. Are you Reza Kianian?"

"Yes, I'm glad you know me."

"I've seen all your movies. I really like you."

"Which one did you like best?"

"Shahrzad" where you were dealing drugs. Shall we take a picture?"

"OK. Take one."

I waited for him to take out his mobile and take a picture. I noticed that he was waiting for me. "Don't you want to take a picture?" I asked.

"But I don't have a mobile. You take one and keep it."

Day – Outdoors – Bahar Street

A distinguished gentleman in a suit and a zipper bag under his arm, about my age, stopped me, said hello, and then added: "I owe you." I was surprised, and said: "Not at all. Rest assured, you don't owe me anything."

He said: "I heard a sentence in one of your movies that really helped me in life. Please allow me to repeat the sentence to you."

I was curious by now and said: "Sure. Please tell me."

He paused for a few seconds and hit his forehead with his hand a few times. He looked in the distance for a while, and said: "It was about young people."

I was anxious to leave. He said: "No, wait please. I'll remember in a minute. Yes. This was it: 'Young people play gooseberry while they're alive; they're the apple of one's eye when they die'."

"Thank you very much. I just learned this from you."

"I learned it from you."

"Well, it makes no difference."

"Then it must have been something else. It was a line in that movie of yours, Water and Fire, Earth and Fire, Fire and Wind ... Something along these lines."

"Don't worry. You'll remember eventually."

He said: "I apologise. When I do remember, where can I find you to let you know?"

Day – Outdoors – Outside My House

A young man who had obviously waited a long time for me to arrive came up to me and said after hello and greetings that he loves the cinema and has seen all my movies. He said: "I have a question for you please, because I've made a bet."

I said: "Please go on."

He said: "This movie "Gavaznha", is it pronounced "Gavaznha" or "Gouvazanha"?

"Gavaznha [The Deer], because Gouvazanha is not a word."

Fanatically, as if he had lost the bet, he asked: "But why?"

"Well, that's what they say. Because when the deer make love, their antlers get stuck together and cannot be untangled; so they die together. This is the point where Faramarz Gharibian and Behrouz die for their friendship." I said.

With tears brimming in his eyes, he said: "I lost. But good for them."

I opened the door and wanted to go in, when he said: "So why wasn't the movie 'Taraj' called 'Gavaznha', because two mates die together in that too."

Night – Indoors – Airport Lounge – City of Ahvaz

We landed at Ahvaz Airport with Habib Ahmadzadeh. We were looking around for a trolley when a staff member saw and recognised me. He came up to us and, following greetings and small talk, I asked: "Excuse me, how come there are no trolleys here?"

After casting a meaningful look at me, he said: "Well, there aren't any as you can see. Are there supposed to be trolleys here just because you're an actor, eh?"

Afternoon – Indoors – Clinic

I was sitting and waiting on the chairs of the clinic for my turn. A mother and daughter were sitting next to me. Several doctors and nurses greeted me within that space of time and, out of the kindness of their heart, said to let them know if there was anything. I'd say thank you and sit back down again. The mother sitting next to me pulled the sleeve of my coat and asked: "What is the specialty of these doctors."

"I don't know."

"Well you should've asked."

"Why?" I asked.

Surprised, she said: "I have a bad back. You could at least ask so I'd know which one to see."

Afternoon – Indoors – "Payam Eraee" Photography Exhibition

We were looking at the photographs with Davoud Amiri. An excited young man approached us eagerly, and said: "Can we take a picture together please, if you don't mind."

And then added immediately: "Well, go see the photos now and then remember to come and take a picture with me in the end!"

Day – Outdoors – Bahar Street

I was on foot. A few high school boys who were just out approached me for a picture. I apologised and said I did not take pictures on the street. By this time, we were at the top of Behesht Alley, which is opposite Imam Sajjad Hospital. A stout nomadic man who had heard our conversation came forward and said: "My son is hospitalised here. Give an autograph for him."

I said: "Come inside the alley." "Sure." He came into Behesht Alley. I signed my name and surname on the piece of paper he provided for his son. The same boys returned to take a picture. As the alley was quiet, I agreed. The nomadic man went to them and said: "Don't you listen? This one said he won't take pictures. He only gave his autograph for a sick person" and left.

Day – Indoors – Outdoors – Bahar Street

We were about to walk into a shop with Davoud Amiri. A man on a motorbike with his wife and little daughter riding pillion arrived and saw us walk into the shop. He also entered and waited for his turn. We said hello and engaged in small talk. When we were finished and about to leave, he said: "Say hello to my wife and kid who're sitting on the bike as you go."

Day – Outdoors – Toronto

I was walking with my son Ali. An elderly lady, who was obviously Iranian, was with her son when she saw me and smiled. She wanted to say hello, but I took the initiative and greeted her. She answered me and said: "Welcome. What are you doing here?" She did not wait for my answer and added: "Why did you come in the cold season son?"

Her son said: "But it's not cold now mum."

The elderly lady said: "You're right. It's cold in the winter. But the cold here never leaves one's bones."

Day – Outdoors – Street

I left Vahdat Hall. I had to dash to Charsou Shopping Centre. It was during the Tehran International Film Festival season which was being held in Charsou.

A young lad approached me and said: "May I take a few minutes of your time?"

"Sure, but I'm in a rush. Please tell me along the way." He accepted and we carried on. I was walking fast and he caught up with me. He explained that he is a playwright and writes screenplays too. He wrote poetry too. Without hesitation, he said: "I want to recite a ballad for you. Breathless, he recited. It was over soon.

"How many couplets was it?" I asked.

"Fourteen."

"As a rule, a ghazal is this size. A ballad is longer."

"What difference does it make. I've written ghazals which are longer than this." He said and began reciting. I cannot remember how many couplets it was. Only that it lasted two red lights when we were at the Hafez-Jomhuri junction…

Day – Outdoors – Opposite Vahdat Hall

I was going to Vahdat Hall parking lot to pick up my car. A

young lad approached me and said: "Where can I get a photography permit?"

"For what kind of photography?"

"You know, photography. To take pictures."

"You don't need a permit. Take your pictures."

"Sir, you don't know where to get permission for filming?"

"Well, it depends. For what?"

"Never mind. Got any new series?"

Northern Iran – Indoors – Boutique

The boutique was really busy. Hayedeh and I were together. After a few hellos and requests for pictures, a man with a crying boy in his arms approached me. We said hello and then he just put his arm around my shoulder and proceeded to take a photo with his mobile. I saved myself and said I'm sorry I don't take pictures in crowded places. He said this kid wants a picture with you. I'm not interested for myself. And the child continued to cry restlessly.

Day – Outdoors – Shuttle Taxi Rank

I sat in the front. The driver was waiting outside to pick up another two passengers to fill up the car in the back and leave. Another driver walked up to him, pointed at me, and said to him: "You've picked up an actor!?" And laughed. Without looking, he pointed at me and said: "There are many of these down our way in "Nezamabad". But there are only two of these around here. This is one of them; and the other one is an old man who walks with a stick." Then he turned to me and asked: "What was his name?"

I said: "Who?"

He said: "The burly guy! The old one! With the stick!"

He was talking about Atash Taghipour.

Day – Indoors– Road to the North – Restaurant

We walked in with the whole family. We sat at a table and waited to give our order. Just as soon as the waiter who came to take our order saw me, he said: "I'm glad to have met you in person by God. I was bored with just watching you in television series."

Day – Outdoors – Narenj Townlet

One of the gardeners in the townlet saw me. After hello and greetings, he finally said: "I've seen your movie. It was really interesting. You come every year, and the kids keep telling me, but I'd never seen it."

"Which one did you see now?"

"The one in which there were two guys and you kept answering back."

"What was it called?"

"Aoooou, what difference does it make! There were two people and you were really good at answering back at them."

Day – Outdoors – Coffee House – Northern Iran

We parked the car and got out to have some tea and rest for a while. We had not entered the coffee house yet when two people came up to me, one of them put his arm around my shoulder and said to his friend: "Snap."

I removed his arm and said: "Hello. You want to take a picture, put me in the picture too." He placed his arm around my shoulder again and said: "You're famous!" And turned to his friend: "Snap."

Night – Outdoors – Hotel Apartments – Northern Iran

We had to spend a few days working by the Caspian Sea in northern Iran to shoot the series "Seven". We arrived at our place of residence at 11 o'clock at night with Mohammad Amin.

We picked up our keys, said goodbye, and went to our respective apartments. I looked around and noticed that there were no tissues, towels, etc. I made a note and went back to the concierge to say what was missing in the room. The concierge looked at me and said: "You're an actor? Cry."

I said: "My dear, it's late at night and I'm not in the mood. Please ask them to bring these for me." I placed the note in front of him and left.

When I was looking for the makeup room early the next morning, he saw and approached me, saying: "Just cry for me. You cry so sweetly in the series."

At Different Times – Talesh

We were spending a few days by the Caspian Sea to shoot the series "Seven". I used to go to Talesh to do my shopping, especially to buy Talesh cheese. I used to wear a mask for Covid-19. But wow! They still recognised me in every shop I went to, and only said a couple of words with a smile: "It's you?"

Day – Outdoors – Village – Northern Iran

We were on location on a bridge in a village in northern Iran to shoot the film "Nowhere, Nobody". During one of our breaks, I was leaning back on the bridge railing with tea in my hand, talking to the locals. One of the local lads who had heard we were filming arrived breathless. He looked around; saw me and approached. He shook hands very politely and said: "I heard you were here. I wanted to meet you in person." Then he turned to the others and said: "Do you know how he is different from the rest?" And went quiet.

The others said nothing. I was also waiting to see what he would say.

He said: "The difference is that Mr Reza is an online action star."

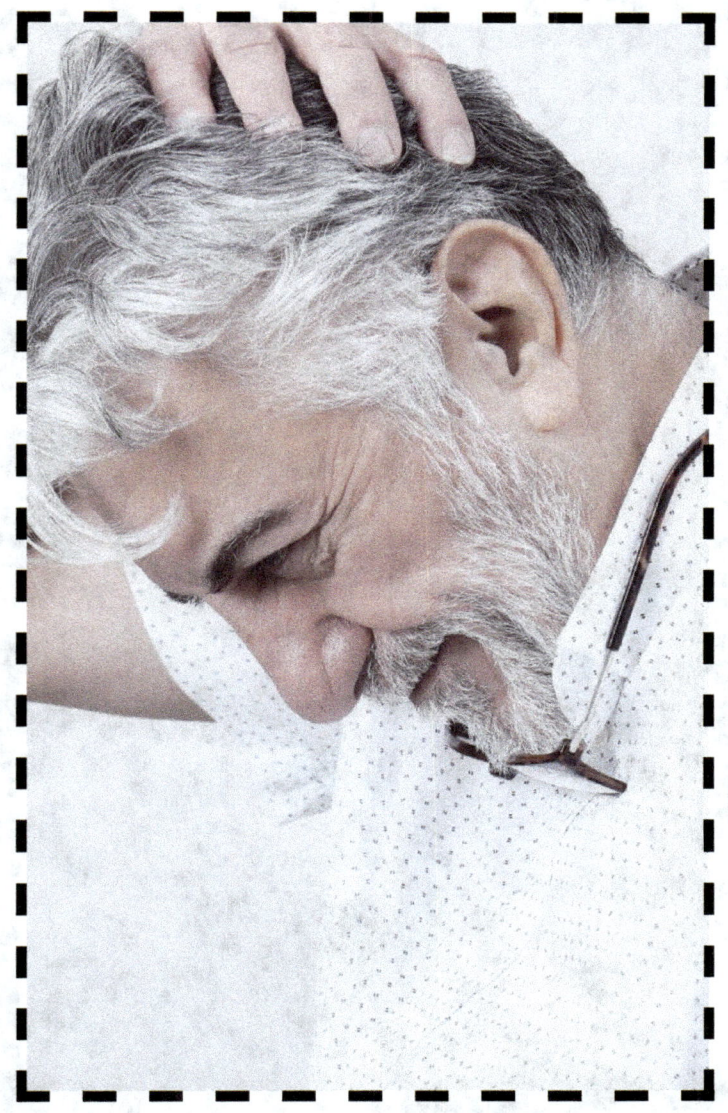

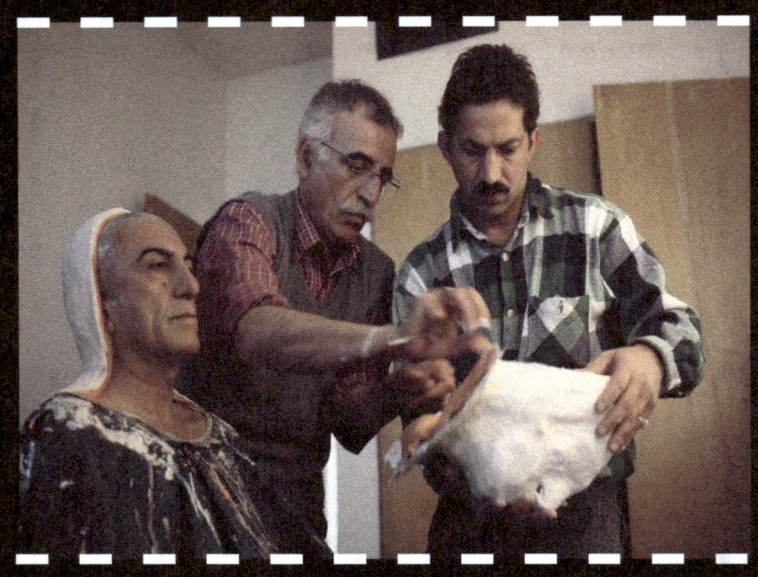

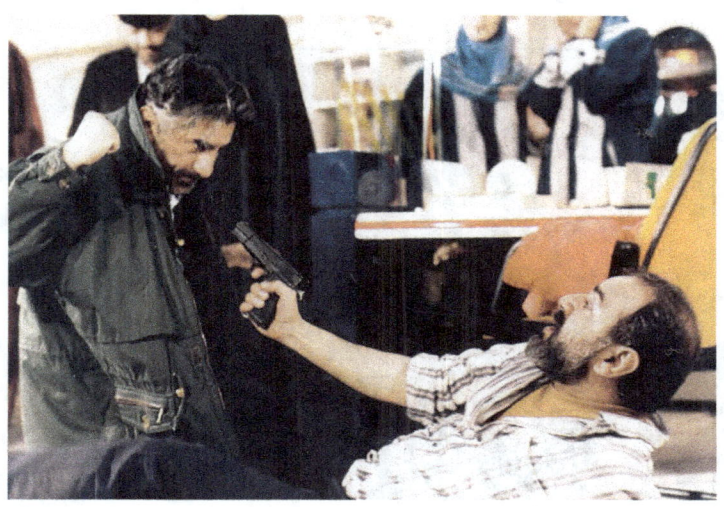

Reza Kianian

Reza Kianian stands out as a prominent and renowned actor in contemporary Iran. His notable achievements in the country include receiving two Crystal Simorgh awards, a Hafez Award, and two Cinema Celebration Awards. Beyond his acting prowess, Reza Kianian showcases his talents as a painter, sculptor, and set designer. This book delves into his encounters with various individuals throughout his life, offering a collection of humorous yet thought-provoking stories that have garnered significant popularity. Reza Kianian's fame and success are a testament to his remarkable talent and dedication.

www.ingramcontent.com/pod-product-compliance
Lightning Source LLC
Chambersburg PA
CBHW072100110526
44590CB00018B/3248